PER STRAND & LENA STORMVINGE

Self-service and Knowledge Success

1:st Edition

Copyright. Per Strand and Lena Stormvinge. All rights reserved 2016.

Published by Per Strand and Lena Stormvinge

No part of this publication may be reproduced, stored in a retrieval system, or transmitted in any form or by any means, electronic, mechanical, phototyping, recording, scanning, or otherwise, except written permission from both authors/publishers.

Limit of Liability/Disclaimer of Warranty: While the publisher and author have used their best efforts in preparing this book, they make no representations or warranties with respect to the accuracy or completeness of the contents of this book and specifically disclaim any implied warranties of merchantability or fitness for a particular purpose. No warranty may be created or extended by sales representatives or written sales materials. The advice and strategies contained herein may not be suitable for your situation. You should consult with a professional where appropriate. Neither the publisher nor the author shall be liable for damages herefrom.

Cover photo: Therese Walve

Edition: First Edition
Printed in United Kingdom, by Lightning Source UK Ltd.
Milton Keynes UK, UKOW06f1624121016

Official site for this book: http://www.selfservicesuccess.com

KCS[SM] is a trademark of The Consortium for Service Innovation.

®ITIL is a registered trademark of AXELOS Limited

ISBN 978-916390042-6

Authors

- **Per Strand** is CEO and co-founder of the international self-service knowledge company ComAround, with over 20 years' experience of implementing efficient knowledge management and self-service he is one of the most experienced people in the field of self-service and knowledge. He has highest-level Knowledge-Centered Service certification and is a certified Help Desk Institute Professional. He is an experienced speaker in leading IT- and support forums.

- **Lena Stormvinge** is a certified KCS Trainer with over 10 years of experience, including implementing cost-effective service solutions, knowledge management strategies, product development and building collaborative teams. Her specialty is helping organizations to better knowledge management strategies through the adoption of best practices methods. Lena's accreditations include the highest-level Knowledge-Centered Service certification and certified Help Desk Institute Professional.

Contents

Part I – Why?   9

Introduction self-service and Knowledge Management   11

Why is self-service increasing in popularity?   20

The growing iceberg and shadow support   26

The shift from perfect to good enough   31

Self-Service means new metrics for your organization   35

Just in time vs just in case   39

The Hero is The King - Not Content   42

The Millennials - Digital Natives   46

Encourage your employees to share their knowledge?   54

How do you evaluate employees without rating them?   57

When information becomes valuable knowledge   59

The key to self-service success is re-use   64

A knowledge tool is an important enabler   73

How many articles do we need to go live with self-service?   77

Part II – How? 91

Introduction to creating the future support organization	92
5 Essential Tips for self-service Success	96
The process for capture, structure, reuse and improve	101
Capture knowledge	102
Structure knowledge	108
Reuse knowledge	114
Improve knowledge	121
Content health	125
Process integration	137
Performance assessment	142
Leadership and communication	149
Marketing	156
Ditches	161
Glossary	167
References and sources	213

Part I – Why?

Understanding and background to self-service and Knowledge Management and the shift in technology and behavior.

Introduction to self-service and Knowledge Management

Basic knowledge and understanding is always the first step towards any change that provides new advantages and increased benefit when compared with the current situation. Without this knowledge and understanding, we cannot see the opportunity or need to develop.

Self-service and Knowledge Management are terms that are more culturally significant than ever, and an increasing number of companies and organizations recognize that there is huge profit to be made for those who succeed in harnessing these terms. Other popular terms that are closely connected to self-service and Knowledge Management are automation, shift left and level zero support or zero level support.

We are asking all those who are interested, to understand what self-service is and what it is that pushes this strong trend forwards. We are particularly keen to ask companies and individuals with some link to a support organization and who need to understand how self-service and knowledge methods like KCS (Knowledge-Centered Service) can affect them; and/or those who need to develop and improve their support and service. The readers will obtain an in-depth understanding **in these areas, as well as** receiving concrete tips and recommendations on how to introduce working methods that utilize the opportunities this will provide.

Self-service and knowledge methodology such as KCS are creating new possibilities to generate real customer value and long term success for service and support organizations and on a higher level for the hole organization. Organizations that see it as a temporary trend and not as something necessary risk losing customers who will get help elsewhere.

It is time to stop viewing self-service as a project or as an initiative. Self-service should be a natural part of almost everything we do, and cannot be separated from other parts of a support or service process.

For a support organization, the development, availability and use of self-service should be just as obvious as supporting their higher goals and core operations. Another reason to take a closer look at self-service and your way of working with knowledge methodology is because users have an increasing number of different options available to find online support, such as through Google – and there is a large gap between an organization's total number of problems and the number of incidents that actually reach service desk. Therefore, in addition to improving how to manage existing incidents, there is great potential to reach more of the issues that, for some reason, are never picked up by service desk.

An improved knowledge flow, plus updated and available self-service can thus reduce the need for alternative solutions.

We have a tendency to focus too much on technology in the early phases, as it is simple, easily-available, is visible and easy to adopt. It is much harder to assess customer requirements or to compare our service with the alternatives offered by competitors. All too often we look for the solution to larger issues and challenges in technology. As technology grows, matures and becomes matter-of-course, we shift our focus to the key question and the actual needs. This is when we approach successful service and begin to achieve a function at a higher level.

Regardless of which support and knowledge methodic we practice customer always has to come first and customer success and customer satisfaction is the primary goal for our efforts.

One successful way to approach this kind of new behavior is to learn from the old way of working, to really understand the basics and what the customer needs. When E-commerce f eks. where at an early stage we regarded it as an entirely new business, and where purely e-commerce businesses sprang up. Now that it has matured, we can see that it is increasingly growing together with physical commerce, and established companies with physical sales have progressed with their e-commerce, they tend to quickly become market leaders and successful in this field.

They simply know their customers, products and understand market needs, regardless of whether the sale is made in a physical store or online. What we learn from this is that it is the same basic driving forces in both instances, and it is very difficult to separate them successfully. They should provide power to each other and create added value, both for the customers and the business. There are always exceptions, but this is the general picture.

This is exactly how self-service and traditional staffed service and support work. As soon as we separate them, they lose power. They are just different distribution types for the same service. When they are linked together in work processes, people and technology, they strengthen and guide each other, leading to faster, better and more efficient support and service. This does not mean that all types of issues should be managed the same way. Some questions are better suited to be solved through self-service and others through manned support.

Many companies make the mistake of allowing their intranet or communication teams to be responsible for and maintain all information within the company, even such information that touches on self-service. The problem with this is the same as e-commerce teams. They are involved in the technology and distribution channels but rarely understand the complexity of the service provided or the customers' requirements.

This is why the support organization should own, be responsible for and manage the company's self-service Knowledge, regardless of whether or not it is made available on the intranet.

Self-service and Knowledge Management are two parts that give each other huge synergy and strengthen each other. They also need each other to function, and in this book we will explain why a key factor to success is to integrate these parts. We will specifically talk about self-service Knowledge and how the popular knowledge methodology KCS can be practiced and help your organization capture, structure, reuse and improve knowledge as an integrated part of your service and support.

A company's or organization's collective knowledge is of greater value as the majority of businesses develop towards more knowledge-intensive business. Today there is a huge need to find ways to get access of and use this knowledge. The companies and organizations that succeed with this will be tomorrow's winners, and will prosper. The companies that don't succeed will find it harder and harder to keep up in increased competition and the constantly growing need for quick access to knowledge.

We will also deal with the key aspect of "what's in it for me?" for the end customer, support agents, management and the entire organization. To convert towards a successful Self-Service and functioning Knowledge process, where the entire organization contributes, we need to be clearly able to present to all target groups our response to the question: "what's in it for me?"

We will deal with self-service primarily from a general perspective rather than a technical one. Self-service is a wide term and we are focusing on it from a knowledge perspective, or self-service Knowledge.

We see how a working method where the entire organization is involved and contributes to the combined knowledge will contribute to better support and supports the overall business value. As a complement to this, more practical and technical self-service functions can also be connected, such as password management, permissions and incident request. These we reasonably view as being on another level.

In terms of what Knowledge Management is, we get as many different answers as people we ask. For you to understand what we mean by Knowledge Management, we will explain and give a brief description.

At a general level, Knowledge Management is about how a company or organization handles, manages, transfers and shares its inherent knowledge.

The purpose of Knowledge Management is to share what we know (ideas, experience and information) so we can improve our efficiency by reducing the need to rediscover knowledge. Structured and functioning Knowledge Management is a key process and enabler for self-service.

Knowledge Management (KM) is formed of three key parts. These are: People, Process and Technology (sometimes known as System or Platform).

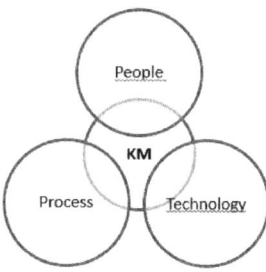

These three parts form the basics of Knowledge Management and all three are required in order for Knowledge Management to work. Without the right processes, neither the people nor the system know what should happen and when. Without the right people, everything stops, as there is no force to drive the implementation and development forwards. Without the right technology, there is no system and technology to obtain the structure needed for success. It is meaningless to try and rank these in order of importance; essentially they are all needed.

Self-service is a concept where - by offering knowledge or services via self-service - we can allow customers and users to solve issues themselves without needing to contact a staffed support every single time.

For the concrete question of "Why?" we primarily find the answer in the measurable positive effects that a functioning self-service provides, and a workplace with knowledge at its center, where the support teams goal is to solve as many customer issues via self-service as possible. Below are some examples of concrete results that this working method creates.

The result is itself a reason to start a knowledge incentive with KCS and self-service:

- Up to 50% case deflection
- 50 - 60% improved time to resolution
- 30 - 50% increase in first contact resolution
- 70% improved time to proficiency
- 20 - 35% improved employee retention
- 20 - 40% improvement in employee satisfaction
- 10% issue reduction due to root cause removal

Our expectations and hope

We (the authors) hope that this book will encourage new ideas, provide useful tips and most of all inspire and create change. We hope to help all those who are thinking of starting a knowledge initiative and providing a functioning self-service and increased customer satisfaction as two of the outcomes. Our experience is that every organization is unique but that there is a lot to learn from what other organizations have already achieved. Please share your thoughts and experience in this area and the content in this book with us at www.selfservicesuccess.com

Thank you for reading Self-service and Knowledge Success.

Why is self-service increasing in popularity?

Technology creates opportunities to offer self-service services within certain areas, which means both a quicker and higher level of service than traditional staffed support. The times when self-service was a cheaper, worse support option are long gone. Good self-service support will add value to staffed support.

Self-service is an enormous force that will completely change the way we are used to giving and receiving service. There are a number of fundamental forces driving us towards an increased degree of self-service. It is partly the extremely rapid development of technology, creating new and better opportunities to allow us to do things we have done before, but in entirely new ways, using new software and hardware. This development is driven by an entire industry, and particularly by market leaders and companies such as Google, Apple, Microsoft, Facebook, and Amazon. It is partly a development where more and more companies are competing in the same field and where the ever clearer competition forces cost-efficient ways to supply services. This is where self-service is a key competitive advantage.

Three fundamental points drive the demand and need for self-service:
- **Development of technology** with new increased opportunities for better service through self-service

- **Increased competition** requires cost-efficient solutions such as self-service

- **Our own improved IT/data maturity** creates a need for quick, simple methods to solve problems independently and obtain service without needing to contact a physical person

A common objection to self-service internally within companies and organizations is that support workers draw the wrong conclusions and say "our users are spoiled, demanding and special, and they prefer staffed support." We are different as individuals, different ages, experiences, knowledge, etc., which means that a number of people will prefer the chance to speak to someone in person. However, this is increasingly a minority, and the problem is that support workers spending the whole day just to have contact with this group who themselves choose to contact a staffed support team, will only reflect a small part of all employees and all the issues that exist in an organization.

A survey carried out by research agency Coleman Parkes in 2014 shows that 91% of customers say they would prefer self-service if it were available and tailored to their needs. At the same time as the support workers persuade themselves that the majority wants to talk to a real person, the staff increasingly Google answers to the questions and turn to their colleagues for help. In an ineffective support organization that is not up to date with this development, not a single member of this growing group is noted as a user.

Surveys clearly show that fewer and fewer of the queries that arise ever reach the service desk. In an organization where the total number of queries successively increases, it can become even harder to define this change in behavior.

Service desk Challenges and user behavior

Much of the development comes from within the business-to-consumer world and it has become standard that this is new technology, and different forms of self-service are being established. Once we have learned to use these new working methods, they are adopted by the business world and become a part of our everyday working life.

If we look at support through self-service, this development has moved fastest within the business to consumer sector. The reasons for implementing this are almost invariably a combination of the above three basic reasons.

As usual, when it comes to different types of changes in our behavior, there is often an inbuilt early resistance. If we have something that works reasonably well, we do not want to risk making anything worse, or we do not consider it worth spending time on investigating if it could be done better. This particularly applies to how we adopt self-service as individuals, both private and in a company.

If, for example, we look at some of the fastest growing areas for self-service on the consumer side, it is e-commerce, gaming, banking and different types of information to the public sector and local authorities that has driven the self-service trend. For example, look at how we, in a very short time, have entirely moved over to self-service in areas such as travel, banking, registering sickness absence, online gaming, etc. Initially, there were many who thought the move to self-service would mean a worse level of service and that it was only being done to increase profit margins in the companies and organizations behind the implementation.

Today, few people would think of booking a trip without being able to go online themselves to make comparisons, see pictures, films, read other reviews, look at alternative package options, etc. And it is the same idea in banking, when bank branches closed down or had reduced opening hours, and the customers were advised to move to online banking instead. Initially there were a lot of protests, but after only a few years there are few people who could even imagine being customers in a bank that didn't offer web or mobile banking.

We will see the exact same pattern within all areas and a functioning self-service is already, and will be, an even clearer requirement from consumers and from employees within the company.

A company's service desk that supports employees does not however experience as clear competition as an external customer service operation. When we dress up as the role of private consumer, surveys show that we think the support we get for goods or services is a key variable in our choice between different options. As an employee of a company it is not likely to choose a job based on the support my colleagues will provide. That is, the external support has an increased degree of visibility in respect of company performance and the last line in terms of happy and repeat customers.

It should be obvious to all service desks that provide support for employees of a company to have the same drive and ambition to always deliver as high a level of service and availability as possible and in a way the customer wants. This is where many companies and organizations work too slowly, with old methods and metrics.

A service desk that has not succeeded in providing functioning self-service will soon loose internal customers to other support channels such as Google or colleagues. In the worst case scenario, unplanned separate support pools will be created, where specialists in specific areas take over the service desk's job role and begin providing support within their area of expertise.

In conclusion, for a service desk to function and survive in the long term, there can only be one attitude: to listen to the customer and create a modern service function where self-service with an updated knowledge base is the core of the support network. Once we as individuals have opened the door to self-service and seen the advantages in terms of speed and increased service, we won't go back to manual services. Self-service and automation of the support process is a huge opportunity for every service desk that understands and takes advantage of this.

The service desk has to transform itself and do the groundwork it takes to change 'the way of working', implement the necessary training and build the right team with members who support and believe in the transformation. Knowledge Centered Service is a great methodology for starting this journey.

The growing iceberg and shadow support

All support organizations are facing significant changes in the years ahead. As previously mentioned, it is new behavior and new technology that is behind the shift. This means both opportunities for us as support organizations if we understand and act on this change to our surroundings, but also a direct threat if we do not understand or do not successfully readjust our support delivery to meet these new needs.

At present, we can see that an increasing number of support organizations are struggling to achieve a sufficiently good level of support and service provision to their organization and customers. Their focus is at the top of the iceberg - they are taking measurements in the same way they have done for the last ten years and they have not changed their objectives to match any changes in circumstances. The effect is that their customers will go elsewhere, and we are seeing an increasing amount of 'shadow support', which is hard to measure and difficult to control.

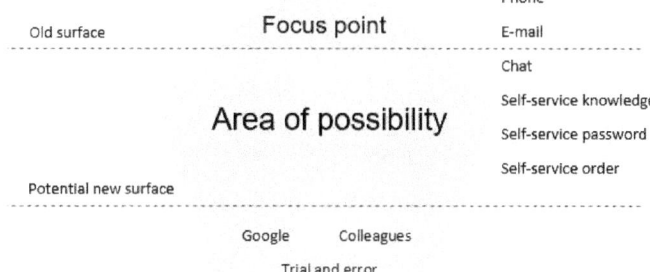

This new behavior and technology mean that we also need to rewrite the needs, objectives and metrics for the support we are to provide. As support organizations, this is where we have a responsibility to convey the image and create an understanding at management level, to indicate that we need to change our old ways of working and therefore also change our requirements and objectives.

We measure activities that are easy to see and measure, which is one of the greatest challenges for many support organizations. We want to describe this in more detail and provide concrete tips on how to take measurements at the right level and highlight new KPIs. These KPIs help you take measurements at a higher level where the focus is not on measuring activity such as incoming calls or call length, but on outcome such as customer satisfaction and **self-service success**, and measure how much your support is costing in relation to your business as a whole.

Most people are surprised at how many issues can be solved via self-service, just as long as it is both introduced and made available correctly. There is occasionally an incorrect idea that self-service will primarily reduce the number of incoming calls and queries. The truth is that only a few issues currently reach service desk, with the majority ending up in one of the other informal support channels we spoke about earlier, such as Google or dealt with by a colleague.

So the problem in the first place is not that we need to change or even reduce the number of incoming cases to a staffed support, but that we do not have a sufficiently long or broad reach within the organization we are supporting. A large number of simpler and recurring issues that previously were dealt with by a staffed support team can and should be directed to self-service, but the key value is created when we increase the service and make the support organization more important and of greater value for the organization. We supply real customer benefits.

What we mean is that a service desk that does not follow the customer's behavior and ignores the self-service trend will slowly lose value and customers will quickly find other ways to resolve their issues and get responses to their queries. The service desk risks a low status from customers, who will eventually view it as insignificant or forced.

This is already happening in some organizations and when management realize this, they quickly come to the conclusion that the service desk is not needed or at the very least does not fulfill its task, which leads to it being scaled down in size or even eliminated entirely. On the other hand, a service desk that understands and uses this opportunity, measures KPIs at the right level and aims for a broad influence within the company and with its customers by utilizing different support channels, will strengthen its value by resolving more issues and achieving more satisfied customers.

Self-service is therefore not primarily about replacing people with databases, but is more the fact that we need to enable self-service; we need to regularly create and develop knowledge articles on the daily support work that is achieved, which will allow us to increase our service and consequently also our value. The basic groundwork in developing knowledge articles should not be done as a project or something additional to what is already being done, but should be woven into the **current incident processes.**

We describe the working method and process needed to develop self-service and knowledge articles in greater depth in the second half of the book.

One way to visualize the challenge and opportunities in achieving a deeper and wider reach is by using the iceberg model. It is very common to place too much focus on the visible top part.

And while we do that, the iceberg is slowly growing beneath the surface. The support and issues that are beneath the surface - i.e. which are never seen - are known as 'shadow support'. If we turn a blind eye to what is going on underneath, we will eventually lose our value as a support organization. At a higher level, defined SLAs (Service Level Agreements) can also contribute to the fact that we are not expected to see the bigger picture, and can prevent a holistic view of the need for support.

So - dare to let go of the SLAs for a moment, and think about what your iceberg looks like; dive underneath and try to see it as a whole. Is it really the top of the iceberg where you should focus your power? Or are the processes at the top adequate and it is perhaps under the surface where significant potential is untapped, both now and in the future?

To put it into practice, the iceberg theory means that many organizations need to spend less time refining their processes and methods which do not fully meet requirements, but have major challenges linked to customers' new behavior, new technology and an increasingly complex environment. With the right attitude, a focus on customer benefits and an organization that is open to change, these can all be significant possibilities to successfully provide an even better level of support to meet the behaviors of today and the future.

The shift from perfect to good enough

The traditional viewpoint that everything should be documented and be perfect has no connection to how we consume information. The organizations that realize this and succeed in creating knowledge management that prioritizes methods for early identification of new issues, turning them into known problems with known solutions - will be winners.

When we work with support and self-service support in particular, time has become an increasingly important factor to consider. The content of the documentation and databases currently generally lives for a brief time. There are always new systems, technology and processes being developed, meaning that we can hopefully find better ways of working. The reason for this is the sheer speed of development in technology; something we have never seen before.

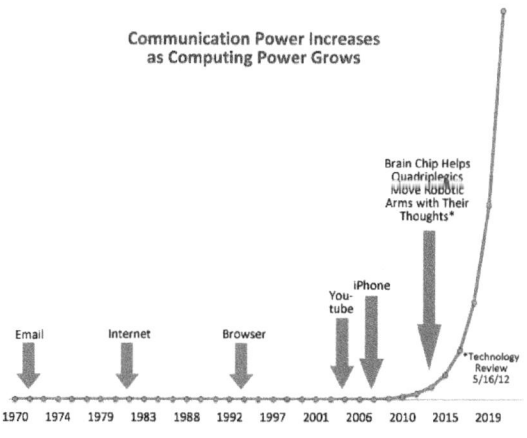

Surveys show that a knowledge article today has an average lifespan of average 60-90 days. It can retain its value afterwards, but it is within the brief period that a clear need exists. With this knowledge, it is logical that it is not profitable to spend too much time in creating perfect knowledge articles for self-service. It is more important to set up a process where we quickly create new knowledge articles as soon as the need arises.

'Just in time' vs 'just in case' and 'Sufficient to solve' is terms used heavily in the knowledge method KCS (Knowledge-Centered Service).

They highlight the importance of the time it takes to create new articles in relation to working proactively to create articles that might be in demand and that the focus is creating knowledge sufficient to solve rather than being perfect.

Why have we been so focused on quality and demanded entirely faultless, proofread and edited knowledge articles? One reason is that we originally used technical documentation and product descriptions as support material. These documentations as a rule have a longer lifespan and must be perfect every time. It can be both financial and legal reasons that are placing significant requirements on mostly perfect content.

When we create knowledge articles in a support organization, we only have one goal, which is to support our customers so that they can solve their problems and continue working. That is, if the article is of sufficient quality for the employee to understand how something works and by reading an article, solves their problem - then our goal has been met. It is therefore time to begin to establish a process where the time it takes to issue new articles is a priority factor in relation to the quality and perfectionism.

In order to get this new working method to function, there are many peripheral factors, and many times we see that a huge cultural shift and understanding is needed to cope with this change. It must be considered as OK that knowledge articles contain minor errors. The most important thing is that the articles explain the bigger picture correctly, rather than the smaller details being perfect. As long as the goal is achieved, then it is adequate. There is then a continuous improvement process, meaning that the articles improve the more they are used. This enables us to also save resources, by not spending too much time on things that customers are not asking for.

Surveys show that as much as 80 percent of all documentation we create in the company is never even used once. With this knowledge, it is easy to understand that we cannot demand perfectionism, but rather we can aim for 'good enough'.

Some concrete tips to succeed: Buy in and explain to management why it important than ever that knowledge articles are perfectly written. How easy or hard it is for people to understand these with time vs quality is dependent on habits and personality. A person who is hot on quality and works to achieve perfect processes and documentation will likely never complete this phase. Their brakes on proceedings will quickly reduce the chances for your support department to pick up any speed.

Finally, prove that the knowledge articles are good enough by simply letting the customer decide. Determine whether or not the customer received the right help. The knowledge articles that the customers do not consider to be any good are those that you can then spend more time on, to improve them so that they are 'good enough'.

Surveys have been carried out where the end client has been asked whether they would prefer access to knowledge articles at an earlier stage but that they are consequently not quality-reviewed and their quality is not guaranteed. 80-90 percent of those questioned preferred access to these non-validated articles and said that they themselves can take responsibility for validation and would prefer to test them at an early stage. This creates good conditions for teamwork where the customer is involved.

Self-service means new metrics for your support organization

It is time to rethink the traditional support metrics that the majority of service desks utilize to measure how successful they are. One critical reason is that the value that support creates cannot solely be measured by the support organization. The true value of the service desk is that it creates real business value for the organization. It is time to stop focusing so much on the activities of the service desk and start focusing on measuring the outcome of the activities.

We want to understand the outcome of the activities and how they are effecting the business. A challenge with measuring new metrics is that we are not used to measuring KCS focused activities like self-service and it is always easier to present information about traditional metrics than to prove that you are creating business value outside the support organization.

The worst part of not measuring the correct metrics is that measuring "traditional" metrics can be counterproductive and employees may embrace the wrong behaviors. Increasingly service desks and support organizations are creating organizational value with the help of a healthy knowledge base that includes an effective self-service system that can be easily utilized by their customers.

When self-service is working really well the result is that a large number of the simple questions get resolved by the users before they become an incident for the service desk to work on. When you deflect the routine and repetitive calls to the self-service system, the service desk team now has the ability to work one more advanced and interesting problems that often take more time to answer.

When an organization successfully implements self-service it can create challenges for measuring traditional service desk metrics. The outcome of implementing self-service is a more effective organization and an engaged service-desk team.

A service desk that only measures traditional metrics, including: first call resolution rate etc, will see their metrics decline as a result of self-service. With a successful self-service solution in place the easier calls are no longer being handed by the service desk. The positive impact on the service desk is that they are freed up to work on more complex calls. This may result in a lower number of cased solved, and a higher escalation rate to 2nd and 3rd level support. The cost per solved case will potentially rice.

This is only an effect of measuring the wrong activities. Using self-service demands measuring new metrics including the ones below. By measuring these metrics, it is much easier to understand the true value your service desk creates and the value it adds to the organization.

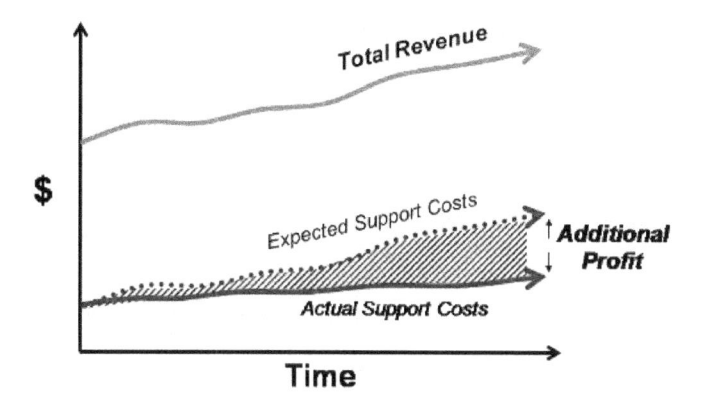

Figure from KCS Measurements Matters, showing support value by expressing support costs as a percentage of revenues.

Recommended new self-service measurements

- **Support cost as a percentage of total revenue** - The ratio of support costs to total company revenue; used to normalize the cost of support in a dynamic environment.
- **Total number of solved case** - Measure the total number of solved incidents including self-service. Self-service is normally increasing the number of solved case with 100-150% if implemented correctly.
- **Customer satisfaction** - How satisfied your customer are with the support environment.
- **Call deflection** - The value of solving customer issues on the web when they would otherwise have opened an incident.
- **Self-service use** - Percentage of customers who use the self-

- **Self-service success** - Percentage of time customers find what they need from their self-service system.

- **Time to publish** - How long it takes new issues to be posted to the intranet or company portal. This is important as a part of the KCS and the knowledge lifecycle.

If your organization is increasing the use of self-service and you struggle with your traditional support metrics, it could be a sign that you are on the right track and that you are creating value for your organization.

You should start identifying You should start identifying which metrics to use and hopefully some of the metrics suggested above will be helpful.

The knowledge methodology Knowledge-Centered Service and The Consortium of Service Innovation describes this process really well and we recommend reading the KCS Measurement Matters document for more information on how to measure the work in your support organization.

Just in time vs just in case

"Creating content is no guessing game".

The traditional way of producing knowledge articles has been to work with it in a project. A project where the most suitable writer, often an expert in the field, is given the task to document all conceivable types of queries that a customer could ask, such as a system or in a process. The material is then proofread, and also sent for translation if needed. The translated material is then proofread again, then everything gets going and the material is published.

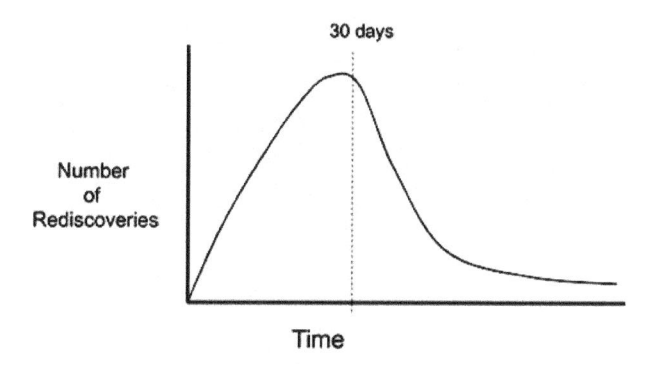

[Graph: Number of Rediscoveries vs Time, peaking at 30 days]

So what is the problem with this way of working? There are several things, including that it has shown itself to be almost impossible to guess in advance the various queries that might arise. That is, we need to have a working method where the end client controls which knowledge articles we create and these should be based on real queries and not on assumptions.

Another problem is that it takes a long time to implement all the sections of this old style process. First an expert is appointed, then they need time to guess which knowledge articles will be needed. It is then proofread by someone who knows the topic and is skilled at finding errors, and finally the entire translation team gets to work, and only then is everything published.

Don't disturb me I'm busy creating loads of knowledge!

Cool, does anyone use it?

However, there are examples of occasions where it is worth being proactive and creating knowledge articles in advance. One example is when we have previous experience of a system and are intending to upgrade or replace it. Then we can make logical and correct assumptions based on our previous experience.

This proactive way of working must always be combined with a working method that involves the customer so that we supplement our proactive knowledge articles with real needs, in the phase where something is used for real. It is seldom worth trying to be too in-depth or too broad when creating proactive material, but a good method is to stick to basic functions and needs that are easier to predict.

The Hero is The King - Not Content

"Of course content is king, but without heroes making it happen there will be no good content"

Your self-service knowledge base is never better than its content. Your ability to set up and maintain content for your knowledge base will be the single most important factor for success. We will give you some basic tactics and ways to make sure the content in your knowledge base meets the demand from your organization.

The best Hero isn't necessary the person writing the best and most valuable knowledge articles but the person who encourage and make it possible for more skilled people to contribute in the knowledge creating process.

Step 1: Choose the Right Content Managers / Coaches - THE HEROES

Your content managers or coaches is by far the most important persons keeping the knowledge base up to date. They should have the qualities and ambitions of a hero. They will make sure the right people are informed, trained and involved in the work of maintaining the knowledge base. Remember: a good coach or content manager does a good job working with the actual content of the knowledge base. But an excellent delegates and makes sure other people contribute. In the early stages, it may be wise for this group of people to be fairly hands-on in order to demonstrate good examples, some short wins and a best practice for others to copy.

Step 2: Track and Analyze Real Usage and Need - ACCURACY

Working with content in a knowledge base is no guessing game. Track real searches and if possible, set automatic alarm functions to notify you if your knowledge base is missing any content. Maintenance, writing new articles and making videos can be time-consuming; you want to be sure your organization truly needs and will heavily use the content you are spending time adding or improving.

Another essential knowledge article category to track is the one your organization does not like. Because you want to improve or remove them as soon as possible. Remember: many reasons may exist for disliking an article, and it is important to understand why. Start by listing your worst articles (the ones with the lowest resolution rate).

Here are a few questions you can use to evaluate why an article is disliked:

- Is the headline right?
- Is the headline matching the rest of the content?

- Is the headline what users search for?
- Are the instructions correct? Do they lead to what your headline says?
- Is it too complex to try to answer a particular issue in a single article? Should it be divided in several articles?
- Is the article in the appropriate format? Are you dealing with a text guide that would be easier to follow as a video?
- Is it too much information? "Less is more", especially when it comes to self-service knowledge articles

Step 3: Use Your Knowledge Base - SHOW THE WAY

Your team should show the way and make sure your service desk team uses the knowledge base as a starting point when solving incidents. Doing so will offer several important benefits. This way your service desk team will be up to date on the contents of the knowledge base and they will automatically look through and improve the articles when needed.

They will also feel a need to add missing articles and they will market the content to the rest of your organization. The popular knowledge management methodology Knowledge-Centered Service (KCS) supports and describes using the knowledge base as a central part of the work performed by the service desk team. The strategy ensures that everyone has access to knowledge in a database and that this is the central method for delivering support.

We cannot expect others to like and use our knowledge base if we do not use it ourselves as support consultants at service desks.

Step 4: Add New Content as Soon as It is Requested - SPEED vs TIME FRAME

Time is crucial when working with knowledge articles. Several studies show that an article will only be an asset to an organization for a limited amount of time.

Knowledge-Centered Service (KCS) best practice indicates that a new article should be available within 90 minutes after the first initial need and that the article will be heavily used the next 30 days, before dropping. With this in mind, we want to establish a process for adding new content that emphasizes time over quality.

If coming up with new articles takes too long, the demand will have passed – or at least peaked – before the article is available.

KCS supports and further explains the concept of focusing on the process and time it takes to add desired articles. To determine which articles to add, use the method described in steps 2 and 3 above. Additionally, make sure a request function is available to end users.

The Millennials – Digital Natives

Whatever we call them, there will continue to come new younger groups of people that has a new relationship to everything that is digital and new technology then previous groups. It can be a challenge but also a source of power.

As we have previously explained, there are many universal trends and factors that are driving the development of self-service, automation and the rapidly growing digitalization in all areas. Our changed behavior and the new generations with younger people who are gradually entering the labor market are contributing factors both for our development and in the need to adjust to the new audience. How does this affect our work with providing world class support and service?

Millennials is an umbrella term with slightly varying definitions and descriptions. Authors William Strauss and Neil Howe have been formally recognized for having minted the term in 1987 at about the time that children born in 1982 began kindergarten and who would later graduate from high school at the Millennium shift in 2000. They wrote about this generation in their book *Generations: The History of America's Future, 1584 to 2069.*

Until now, most of us who are in various business management positions and who participate in making decisions about processes, methods and tools have not been Millennials or born as digital natives. We have needed to constantly challenge our learned behaviors and devote considerable time to trying to convert our old analog technologies and methods into those that are more digital to utilize the opportunities provided by digitalization.

We have succeeded relatively well and despite the difficulties, we have created much of the foundation of the digital solutions utilized by those we refer to as the Millennials. The big difference now is that the Millennials have been born into the digital age, and consequently, they do not need to convert analog things into digital since digital is the norm.

All who have younger children know how they can be swallowed up by the digital world and how digital is the new norm. It will be interesting to see how the new generation – born in the digital age and in a world where access to the Internet, apps, social media, video communication and e-commerce is taken for granted (in most parts of the world) – further develops digital solutions.

How will we be affected when the digital natives grow up and enter the labor market? And how will we succeed in meeting their needs for support and service? How can we utilize their superior abilities in exploiting the technology in entirely new ways – in contrast to what we others have done in the past – to do our utmost in converting from the analog to the digital?

From a longer perspective, the contemporary generations after the Millennials will be even more at home in the digital world, with the Internet and social media, and due to this, the rate of development is progressive and it is just now beginning to gain momentum. It will take some time before those we refer to as Millennials fall behind and need to adopt an even greater degree of digitalization on a level that we now have difficulty in foreseeing.

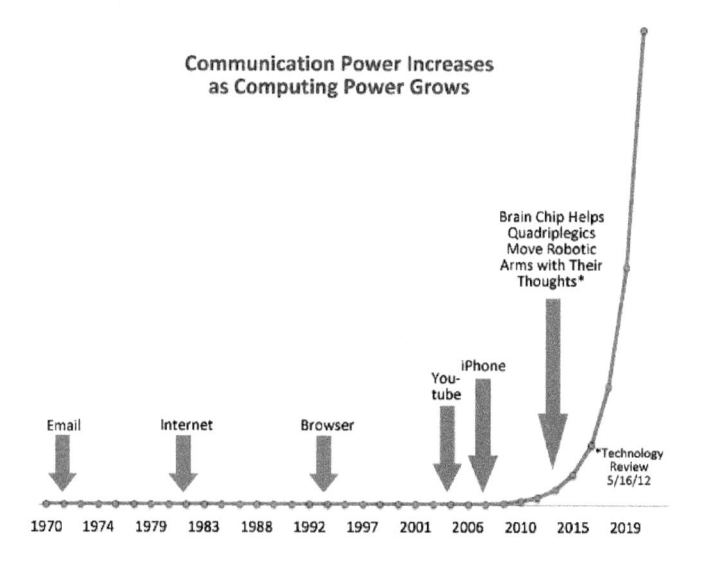

**Communication Power Increases
as Computing Power Grows**

| Email | Internet | Browser | You-tube | iPhone | Brain Chip Helps Quadriplegics Move Robotic Arms with Their Thoughts* | *Technology Review 5/16/12 |

1970 1974 1979 1983 1988 1992 1997 2001 2006 2010 2015 2019

The digital natives do not see it as better service having the opportunity to call and speak with a person at a support department rather than being able to quickly find the answer themselves, when they like and in their own way. They probably do not much care either as to where they find the answer since the boundaries for businesses, brands and social platforms are only digital demarcations that are being gradually eradicated.

This entails that we should work more to keep them in the company's social sphere in support situations. If I cannot find the answer in my own organization, I'll quickly accept help from somewhere else. The alternatives are many and more easily accessible than ever.

Something we must realize is that if we cannot offer smart, accessible and proactive solutions, they will go elsewhere, and in the best event, bring their own solutions and networks back with them. It is very likely that more and more are building their own networks outside the workplace, where there is trust and where they feel a sense of belonging.

It is our experience that organizations that succeed with establishing good self-service are also good at involving younger employees in developing solutions. This provides a partially new way of viewing the technology and contributes to understanding what is important for the new younger audience. Those who succeed best are those that have a breadth in working with self-service and knowledge so that both younger and older more experienced people join in developing the support organization's solutions. This also applies to day-to-day management.

Here are some general characteristics exhibited by the Millenniums that are good to keep in mind when we develop our support and service organization:
As always, trying to categorize and generalize various groups is risky, and obviously not all Millennials have the same relationship to the digital world.

But as a group, we can consider the following as worth taking into consideration when we build the future's service organization.

- Born into the digital age, they can easily see how the technology can be utilized and support the goals.
- "Good enough" is a matter of course. Not the same view on quality, which benefits them from a KCS perspective, for example, where the goal is "good enough to resolve a problem".
- Knowledge committed to memory is not that important. What is important is access to knowledge.
- Digital communication is valued as highly as personal communication IRL.
- The digital is not an alternative, it just IS.
- If solutions are obsolete and undeveloped, they go unused; in other words, we cannot force bad solutions on the Millennials.

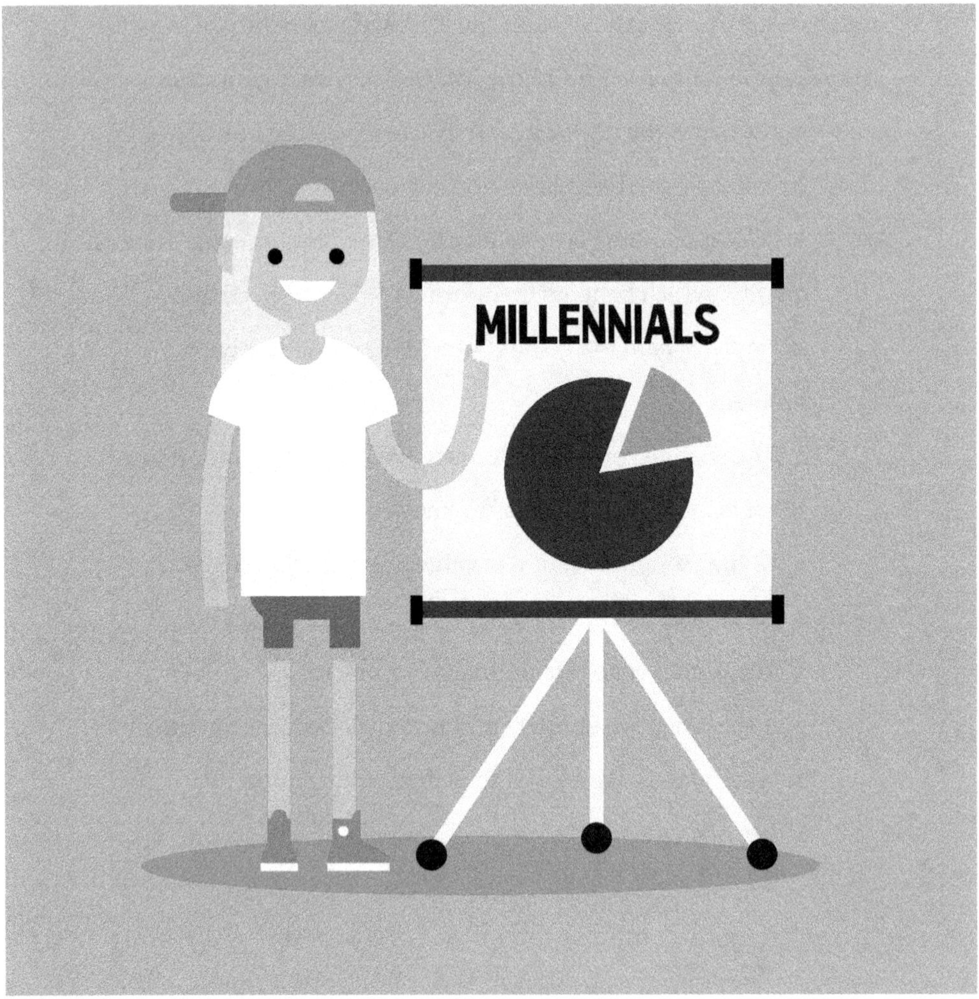
MILLENNIALS

Summary

Millennials is a term that refers to younger people will gradually enter the labor market and who have a completely different relationship to the digital. For them, digital solutions and modern technology are taken for granted and we need to adapt our way of providing service for this and even involve younger people in digitally developing our solutions.

Are you encouraging your employees to share their knowledge?

Companies have in the past been suffering because the people that are sitting on the information has been uneager to share it. As a result of this, colleagues have had trouble accessing the knowledge they need in order to do their job. Luckily, this trend is changing.

In today's knowledge-based work environment. Much of what we need to know we learn from others' experiences. So how do we encourage our employees to share their knowledge?
Here are a few ways you can encourage knowledge sharing within your organization.

Coaching. Each employee needs a mentor or a coach. Someone who can help them succeed within the organization, give input to their daily work, and guide them in adapting the company's best practices. A licensing system when the employee gets to demonstrate their personal growth, can be an excellent tool.

What's in it for Me? Is the question you, as a manager, need to answer. Personal context is usually the first filter we use to evaluate the environment, and this is especially true when we're asked to participate in some sort of change.

Rewards. Reward your employees for contributing to valuable information. Recognition is one of the internal motivators, and by recognizing your employees, they will be motivated to contribute, collaborate, and identify new opportunities.

Feedback. Continuous feedback as a natural part of the job is important for the employee's motivation, satisfaction, and performance. When an employee is motivated by feedback in the form of, for example, evaluations and recognition schemes, they will behave in certain ways to obtain attractive appraisals. Just this drive to motivate knowledge-sharing.

Integrations. Make it easy for your employees, so they can do what they do best. Helping the customer. Organizations are shifting toward work that is more specialized and adaptive. Many have implemented a knowledge-based tool in order to ease the support. Once the knowledge tool is in place, how can you integrate it with other systems, and make it easy available for both customers and team-members?

Encourage vicarious learning. People often hesitate to ask others for help or advice because it requires admitting they don't know something important. So instead they work in isolation, redoing something that their colleagues may have already done or making similar mistakes.

Acknowledge people what engage in interactive learning and recycle (rather than reinvent) knowledge. Encourage an open-door environment that welcomes employees to seek or share knowledge.

Training. Getting outside help and inspiration is a great way of adapting the knowledge sharing strategy. Management often see the need to undertake effective education and training in order to develop their knowledge-sharing culture in their organization.

Companies are sitting on far more knowledge and expertise than they realize. Creating the conditions that enable coactive vicarious learning is a central way to bring out the best a team or organization has to offer.

As Lew Platt, the former chief executive of Hewlett-Packard (HP) said, "If only HP knew what HP knows, we would be three times more productive."

How do you evaluate employees without rating them?

More and more companies move away from the traditional ratings-based performance model in the organization. It makes sense to focus on goals instead of activities. You want your company (and staff) to grow and develop, and in order to do so, you need to focus on the right things.

Measuring activities will give you an unfortunate result as your staff will focus on achieving just that. What you are asking for and nothing more. For example: If you are measuring your support staff on how many new articles they have written a month, you will get a lot of articles. But when you start analyzing the content, you would most likely see that the quality level is low and that there are many duplicates.

In order to receive the best possible result, you need to move away from the traditional rating-based performance model. The new way of measuring performance is setting goals, planning growth, and measuring (both customer and employee) satisfaction levels.

You want to empower your staff, invest in their personal development, and encourage them to trust in themselves. Measuring your staff on goals sets clear expectations in a process without ratings.

Performance meetings are more positive, and the employee will tap into their internal motivators as they can see that their work has a purpose.

Performance and engagement are strongest when employee feel supported, guided and are receiving coaching, as well as have a higher level of ownership for the process. This again, will lead to a higher level of engagement, a new openness to creativity, as well as personal growth and satisfaction.

As Accenture's CEO Pierre Nanterme told the Washington Post when they decided to get rid of annual performance reviews and rankings:

"The art of leadership is not to spend your time measuring, evaluating. It's all about selecting the person. And if you believe you selected the right person, then you give that person the freedom, the authority, the delegation to innovate and lead with some very simple measure."

When information becomes valuable knowledge

Information becomes knowledge when it gains a particular value with the recipient and they act based upon it.

We hear daily that knowledge is modern companies' and organizations' primary asset. More and more businesses are building up their specialization and core products around the knowledge that the employees have. Increased specialization is seen in all areas, and a significant contributing force is the rapidly increasing international competition that companies meet to an ever-increasing degree. It is now easier for the purchaser to evaluate services and products way outside country borders thanks to the internet and increased digitalization.

For most companies, this is an advantage, but also means that competition is clearer and purchasers can simply compare similar products and services, regardless of where the company is based. This means that the winners are those who cope being compared with competitors or substitutes from an international perspective. As a rule, it is the employees' knowledge and specialization that is key, both for contributing to the company's development of a leading product and service, but also in the delivery where knowledge and experience in some cases are just as important as the physical or digital product.

All companies and organizations need to have a functioning system in order to capture, structure and distribute the knowledge that is held by all staff within the business. This is not a quick project solved within a few months, but is about a new viewpoint on the knowledge and teamwork where all employees in a company understand the value of the combined knowledge and also have the correct resources to manage this project work.

It is also important to understand the difference between knowledge assimilation as it has happened historically and where it is more characterized by information collection and documentation and practicing a knowledge methodology that means all employees are simply involved and contribute to the creation of a knowledge database that is accessible to the entire organization.

An essential factor is time, and when methodology such as Knowledge-Centered Service clearly shows that when a new query reaches a support organization, several people will also have the same issue, and even after only 30 days, the number of recurring queries is significantly reduced.

We also know that as much as 80% of all knowledge that is documented using earlier methods is never used, not even once. That is to say, only 20% of what we have documented will ever be looked at again.

Obviously we do not have limited resources, and with this knowledge, we need to change our methods of collecting, structuring and distributing this knowledge, so that we can quickly obtain and make available the responses to common queries and use less manpower on its quality. Neither is knowledge something that is completed, but is developed with the company, its employees and its surroundings in a constantly ongoing process. We must begin by aiming for 100% quality, with the understanding that there is no such thing when documenting knowledge over time.

It is also important that knowledge is collected through teamwork from employees, specialists and the support organization. What is information and what is knowledge will vary depending on who is the recipient of said information/knowledge. This means that it is hard - if not impossible - for one person to determine what is knowledge to another person.

For an office worker in San Francisco, data and details from a 5-day weather forecast can be interesting information but nothing more. To a wine producer in nearby Napa Valley, the same forecast can be incredibly important business-related knowledge. A difference in definition between information vs knowledge is that information becomes knowledge if it has such a particular content or value that I then do or do not act on.

What for one person is very important knowledge is for another merely information. This is why there is no answer to what, for a company, is the 'right' knowledge. The knowledge method must therefore be based on everyone contributing and a key question is how successfully the knowledge is gathered up and then structured, and how well it can be reused and distributed. It is also beneficial to be aware that the key element is not always knowing why something happens or doesn't happen, but rather to share knowledge on how to solve a particular problem. For example, if you drive a car, you need a certain knowledge of the car's basic movements and the rules/laws in place to reduce the risk of an accident when using the car. But that doesn't mean that you need to understand exactly how each part of the engine works.

You probably only know how less than 10% of the car's advanced technology and functions work at a deeper level. If something goes wrong with the car, you need sufficient knowledge to solve the problem or get help from a specialist to do so. This is exactly the same way a company's internal information and knowledge works. Many previous knowledge methods demand complete documentation of all the knowledge and functions in an organization. The problem with this is that it is an enormous amount of comprehensive documentation which must then be maintained and stored, which requires huge resources. Neither will the documentation be available, as it is too comprehensive and more in-depth, rather than being at a level that helps solve common problems or provides answers to common questions.

One effect of this is that many companies have spent numerous hours on documentation but at the same time this has not created any positive effect on how successfully the knowledge is reused and how it solves problems quicker if they reoccur with another employee.

The approach by Knowledge-Centered Service is by developing knowledge articles based on actual queries in an organization, making the focus on reusing knowledge and differentiating between 'known problems' and 'new problems', making available and together developing all the knowledge within the organization. More on how this is achieved is available to read in the KCS documentation and the courses on the subject.

The key to self-service success is understanding the value of re-use

Perhaps the most important understanding for both individuals and teams wanting to succeed with self-service is to understand how incredibly central and decisive the actual re-use instance is; that is, to re-use the knowledge.

It is an absolute prerequisite and we could even go so far as to say without re-use, there is no self-service. The opposite, therefore, is that success of functional knowledge sharing and self-service is a given. So instead of asking the question 'How do we create a successful self-service tool that increases service and also reduces costs of providing support?', we should ask 'How do we create a communal knowledge database where knowledge is re-used and improved through the day-to-day work?'

Much of what we go through in general is about how we create a communal knowledge database or platform for knowledge where we re-use and share. A knowledge article that is reused must, of course, function and solve a problem. The re-use must be supplemented with key figures such as degree of resolution and customer success. Thinking of how important re-use actually is, and how closely linked it is with the success of self-service, it also functions as an important key figure to measure and develop.

The degree of re-use is also a good indicator of how mature a self-service organization is. At an early stage, before we have created a knowledge base, the scope of re-use of knowledge is small. The majority of issues within an organization are new and lack knowledge articles.

An organization that works using KCS has the routine of documenting all new problems, after which they go to a support representative. After some time, the majority of all the problems have recurred and been documented - now 'known problems' and contain a suggested solution and problem description in a knowledge article.

It is at this stage when the database becomes relevant and more comprehensive that it begins to gain significant value for the organization when used correctly. Initially it is the support that re-uses the content, but after support has verified the knowledge articles and had confirmation that they have solved the problem, they can be published and made available for the whole organization via self-service.

It is now that it gets interesting to measure the extent to which the articles are re-used, both within the support organization and as self-service, by the rest of the organization.

In order to get a knowledge article re-used, there are some points which have proven to be particularly important. They are:

- **Need** - That the article meets a need, that is, several people have a need for an answer that the article content can provide.
- **Design** - That the article is correctly designed, with a heading, general text content and metadata that makes it searchable.
- **Time** - That it is created and made available in good time, that is, at the same time as the need arises within the organization.
- **Availability** - That it is published externally and made available for the target group.

In addition to these four, one basic condition is that the knowledge database is available in its entirety and has been marketed to the target group.

What we mean is that the four above sections are equally as important but the ones which stand out and are key to focus on in this context are the first two, Need and Design. Time and Availability are obviously important too, but there are good methods and the entire KCS methodology is about how an organization creates value by focusing on capturing need directly when it first arises and what the process looks like to make this available. Let's take a closer look at the first two - Need and Design.

Need. If we successfully create knowledge articles that meet the needs of the target group and if we successfully describe functioning solutions for the target group's problems, we have a great starting point to achieve self-service success and a high degree of re-use of our knowledge articles.

The best way to identify these problems is by asking the target group, which can be done in various ways. The obvious, and perhaps most important, way is by checking which queries are coming in to the service desk through the various contact methods, such as phone, mail, chat and as a matter raised by the target group themselves directly. This would have been sufficient if the objective had been to provide support via the standard support channels.

However, self-service can differ somewhat, simply because it is self-service. It has been shown that for certain types of problems, we are happy to turn to some form of self-service to find a solution, and do not want to contact a staffed support desk for the issue. And vice versa - for other types of issues, we would far rather speak to a human being. With this in mind, it is key to supplement the method of identifying new articles with what we should have in our self-service knowledge database.

Here are some successful and efficient methods of identifying new knowledge that we have discovered:

- Measure and analyze the standard channels, that is, which issues are coming in via phone, mail, chat, case management, etc.
- Measure and analyze actual usage in the self-service knowledge database. What are the users searching for? What are users looking at? What patterns are there in their usage? When is there the chance to be proactive - for example, during roll-out of new software and other changes in the IT environment.

- Close dialog with different sections of the organization in order to more quickly act on new needs and also gain a consensus on expectations and who is doing what.
- See what other 'similar' organizations have as good examples of functioning knowledge that can be borrowed from. This is particularly applicable in the public sector where similarities are often significant. However, there is also a lot of experience to mine within the private sector.

Design. How we design a knowledge article can be considered a simple detail, but has shown itself to be incredibly significant for determining the degree to which it is re-used.

The design is also something that we can influence to a considerable degree, and it is up to us to create the most optimally designed knowledge article as possible. We should also bear in mind when creating a new knowledge article that we want it to be re-used and how do we design it to be so?

It is largely fingertip sensitive and difficult to define an exact template which works for all knowledge, but a clear and good heading to describe what the article is about, from a user's perspective.

A standard technique is to finish the article and when we know what it will contain and what the solution is, then we will add the heading as a final step. This gives us the best chance to obtain a good, relevant heading.

Another technique that works well is to allow several knowledge articles that are all symptoms of the same problem or error. By doing this, we have a user's perspective. If, for example, we think of several users having the same problem of being unable to print, and are asking for a solution. We will quickly see that the issue is to do with the network, and we would write a new article with the heading: *Connect to the network*. This article would be very hard to find for a user having printing issues, and it is highly unlikely that the user would even associate the article with their problem unless it showed up in a self-service search. An article with the heading: *Resolve the printer problem* would probably feel more relevant. As there are users who understand that it might be to do with the network, there may be the need for two different articles that are both symptoms of the same problem, and this may be the best solution.

These articles can easily be linked to each other to offer more information for those who would like it.

The key to a high degree of re-use is to put yourself in the user's shoes or perspective, and keep it as simple and brief as possible. For example, how many people would even choose to look for the answer they need deep within technical documents written by technicians for technicians?

What we have described above about re-using knowledge is primarily focusing on self-service and it is therefore the person who needs a problem solving who is our target group. This is where profit is at its maximum, when self-service works and the knowledge articles are therefore re-used. The upside is considerable, both because there is no need for additional people to help resolve an issue, as a knowledge article is re-used with self-service, but also because the opportunity is unlimited - that is, self-service can be used to solve a huge volume of problems, volumes which a staffed service desk would never come close to achieving, and primarily at an entirely different cost level.

The second type of re-use is when knowledge is re-used within service desk. This also has significant value for two reasons. Firstly, because it is almost impossible for one person in one service desk to have sufficiently in-depth and broad knowledge within all the areas expected of a service desk capacity.

A knowledge database thereby ensures that everyone working within service desk can simply create and re-use solutions to known problems. The second significant gain with this internal use of knowledge is that the quality of responses is greater, as the result is a service desk that gives the same response to the same issue no matter who responds to the query. That is to say, knowledge does not remain trapped in one person's head, with that person providing a solution to the issue to the best of their ability and previous experience.

Internal use of knowledge is also an effective way of transferring it between the individuals working on a service desk. After some time, a specific knowledge article will contain and represent these people's combined expertise and best practice in combination with a proven solution and function. It is at this stage that an article is normally published externally to also allow it to reach a wider public.

However, it is important to highlight this internal exchange of knowledge, as service desks will see a huge boost and an increased degree of resolution, more satisfied customers, etc. even as early as when this internal knowledge is shared within service desk.

A knowledge tool is an important enabler for successful knowledge management

The right tool supports the chosen method and reduces the need to develop workarounds. It also encourages users to follow the correct methods through having the right flow and functions.

Choosing the right tool for the work with knowledge is important and we often underestimate the difference between the various tools. The working methods and the people are more important than the system and tools, which in itself is correct, but we mean that the tools are not far behind in level of importance.

If you choose to work with the KCS knowledge method, it is even more important to choose a tool that supports the method in a natural way, and where the tool is designed so the natural way of using it leads to the same behavior that the methodology recommends.

We are, of course, slightly biased when it comes to knowledge tools, but we also have a unique insight into the pitfalls when estimating the importance of a good tool. A good knowledge tool can be seen as a good facilitator in the work between knowledge and self-service.

A question we are often asked is where in the tool and system ecosystem we should place a knowledge tool. As knowledge in a company or organization is almost always one of the greatest values, it is important to treat this knowledge cleverly. It is compiled in some form of knowledge database and needs to then be able to be distributed and linked to other important systems.

We recommend that all companies and organizations have a separate system to compile the company's greatest value, the combined knowledge, in a pure knowledge tool. This is where you have to compile the most important information, and it is worth having a specialized tool intended solely for this purpose, to compile, structure and distribute this information. It can be compared to the majority of people using different systems for CRM, intranet, external websites, etc. They are specialized and good at different things.

One of the most important properties in this knowledge tool should be that it builds on modern, scalable and open technology and that it is easy to integrate and link this knowledge core to other tools within the organization, such as the case management system, intranet, CRM, etc.

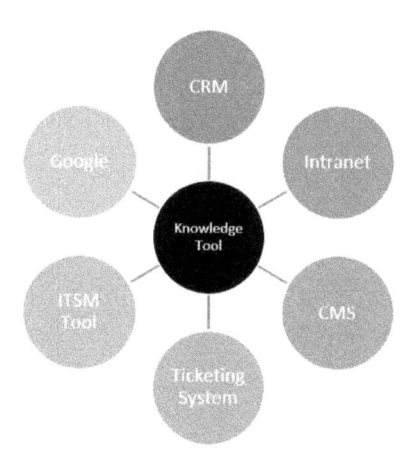

One consequence of having a separate specialized knowledge tool and, for example, not using inbuilt modules in other broader tools, is that you do not need to replace the knowledge tool and - in the worst case - also change the methodology around the knowledge simply because you have chosen to replace your intranet or case management system, for example. The third and final reason for wanting a specialized knowledge tool is purely because it is a specialized knowledge tool.

If your company is in an early stage of maturity and simply needs to get going, an integrated tool will suffice for a while, but to move from OK to good or very good, you will need a specialized tool. We can compare this to connecting cinema-style surround sound to a TV. The TV's own loudspeakers do the same thing - i.e. that they provide sound - and if you simply want to tick that off the list, then you can stop there.

But if you want a better, louder and more comprehensive soundscape, you need to connect a specialized sound system with external speakers. The solutions are theoretically similar, but the experience and result are markedly different.

No inbuilt TV sound can match up with even a mid-range specialized sound system that is designed and optimized for one thing - to deliver great sound. So, since the title of the book is self-service and Knowledge Success, and is aimed at companies and organizations that want to achieve exactly that, we recommend that everyone finds a specialized knowledge tool to integrate with your 'TV' (i.e. your ITSM/case management tool) and let the system simplify and guide you in your work towards self-service and knowledge management.

How many articles do we need in order to go live with self-service?

In order to succeed with self-service, the customers - that is, the people who are looking for answers to their queries through the self-service system - must at least occasionally find what they're looking for. One question is therefore what is the minimum hit rate of how often they need to find answers to their queries and how comprehensive an article database actually needs to be in order to launch a self-service system to customers. We don't want visitors to 'come through the door' and get a bad first impression!

For example, we have seen examples both where self-service is launched too early, and where there is insufficient content to meet the needs of users and customers. In these cases, this is a poor start and it is hard to turn a poor start around if visitors feel that their needs were not met. We have also seen examples of launches where the content is overworked and the attempt to guess what users will search for has been over-ambitious and too far removed from reality.

These attempts are expensive, both because unnecessary time has been spent identifying the need in detail (which is impossible to do), and also that they often delay the launch of the self-service system.

It can also create unreasonable expectations for users to be satisfied and if they are not, the feeling is immediately one of failure.
It is also seldom a good thing to make guesses that are too far-reaching, as they are rarely what is expected. This is due to the fact that users often live in another world to those who are trying to guess which questions will be asked. This is down to changes happening very quickly, for example, changes to the company or product environment where the rate of change is so great that the demand has passed after only a short period and becomes wholly uninteresting shortly thereafter.

So the main requirement to succeed is to think long-term, but also understand that first impressions are important, and users cannot be confronted by an empty self-service database. In order to succeed in the long-term, it is therefore most important to focus on working methods and routines to ensure that those working with the self-service database can quickly update it with new content as soon as new queries come in from the organization, as well as to find ways of constantly improving the existing content.

A basic factor for success is working with a view that knowledge articles are not 'finished' and where the organization understands that these articles continuously change both significance and form depending on the organization and new additional knowledge that can be used to make them clearer, better and perhaps easier to find with new search words for use by customers.

How many articles are needed for success in self-service? The 100 rule or 50 percent hit rate!

In order to try and answer the question of 'how many articles do we need to successfully launch a self-service system?', we can use a formula we have created, to assess what is sufficient.

To begin with, we can use the general rule that if customers find the answer they need in 40-50% of cases, it is likely they will return and use the self-service database again. This is industry standard for self-service success (see Service XRG for the survey). This means that if we cover at least 40-50% of the need, and can provide good responses to these queries, we have a good chance of having enough articles to be able to launch. We can then condense the question down to 'how many articles do we need to cover 40-50% of the requirement?'.

We have created real statistics and analyzed figures from five mature self-service organizations. We have primarily seen what the relationship between volume of number of queries in the self-service knowledge database looks like and the relationship between recurring and different queries. For example, it would be very simple if one (1) individual question and knowledge article in the knowledge database represented the entire volume and all queries. It would be sufficient to identify that one and have it available.

Obviously it doesn't look like that, but we were interested to see the division of queries amongst the hundred most popular knowledge articles in the self-service database. The fact that the articles at the top should be used more was a given, but the issue was how much more? Are the knowledge articles in a top 100 list equally popular and used equally as much, or is it the 10 most popular at the top that account for 90% (10-90) of usage, or what does it look like.

These are real figures from five different organizations and their self-service usage. They operate within different industries, are different sizes and are relatively evenly distributed (3 to 2) between private and public sector. The time period we measured was 30 days.

Conclusion

If you don't have the time or patient to go through the different examples that follows from different organizations, here is the conclusion.

The conclusion is therefore that hundreds of knowledge articles are entirely sufficient in a self-service knowledge database, on condition the system has done a good job in identifying which articles have been requested. A further conclusion is that if we are not successful in finding a good way to identify the key articles, we risk ending up in a situation where we simply guess and write thousands of articles without any successful launch. Here, relevance is considerably more important than volume.

Organization 1:

The organization had 1,002 queries in the self-service database, spread across their 100 most popular articles. Their top 100 list saw each article re-used an average of 11 times.

- The 3 most used articles made up 11% of the queries.
- The 10 most used articles made up 29% of the queries.
- The 25 most used articles made up 52% of the queries.

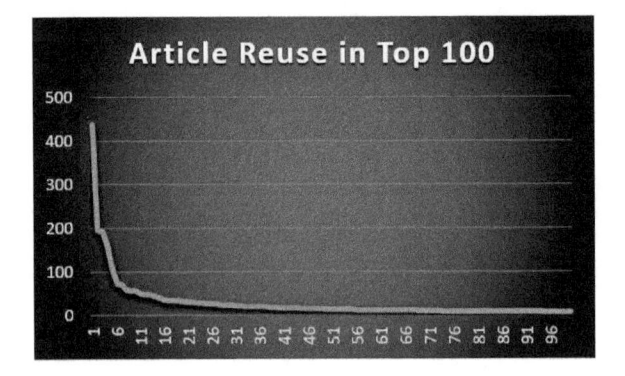

Article Reuse in Top 100

The ten (10) most used articles accounted for around a third (29%) of the queries and usage on the top 100 list. 25-52 relationship.

Organization 2:

The organization had 2,548 queries in the self-service database, spread across their 100 most popular articles. Their top 100 list saw each article re-used an average of 25 times.

- The 3 most used articles made up 36% of the queries.
- The 10 most used articles made up 49% of the queries.
- The 25 most used articles made up 66% of the queries.

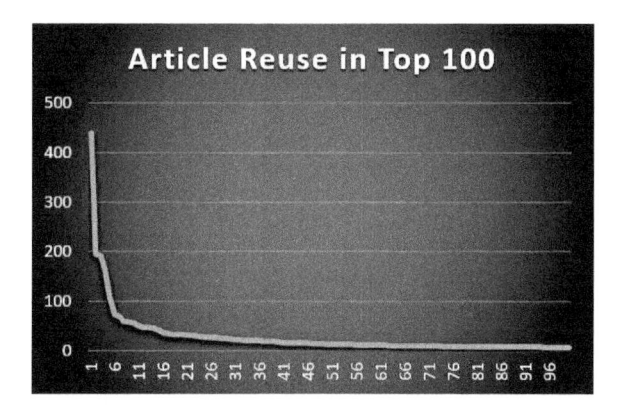

The 10 most used accounted for around half of the queries (49%) and usage on the top 100 list. 10-49 relationship.

Organization 3:

The organization had 2,857 queries in the self-service database, spread across their 100 most popular articles. Their top 100 list saw each article re-used an average of 29 times.

- The 3 most used articles made up 29% of the queries.
- The 10 most used articles made up 49% of the queries.
- The 25 most used articles made up 68% of the queries.

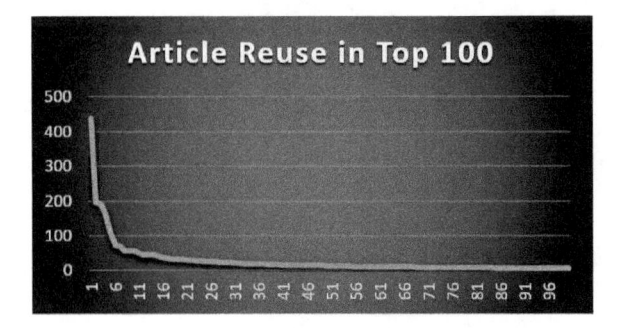

Article Reuse in Top 100

The 10 most used articles also accounted for around half of the queries (49%) and usage on the top 100 list. 10-49 relationship.

Organization 4:

The organization had 16,009 queries in the self-service database, spread across their 100 most popular articles. Their top 100 list saw each article re-used an average of 160 times.

- The 3 most used articles made up 32% of the queries.
- The 10 most used articles made up 64% of the queries.
- The 25 most used articles made up 80% of the queries.

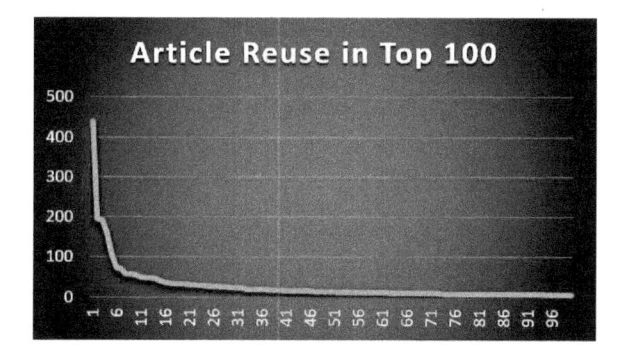

With this organization, the 10 most used articles accounted for 64% of the queries and usage on the top 100 list. 10-64 relationship.

Organization 5:

The organization had 1,928 queries in the self-service database, spread across their 100 most popular articles. Their top 100 list saw each article re-used an average of 19 times.

- The 3 most used articles made up 50% of the queries.
- The 10 most used articles made up 79% of the queries.
- The 25 most used articles made up 88% of the queries.

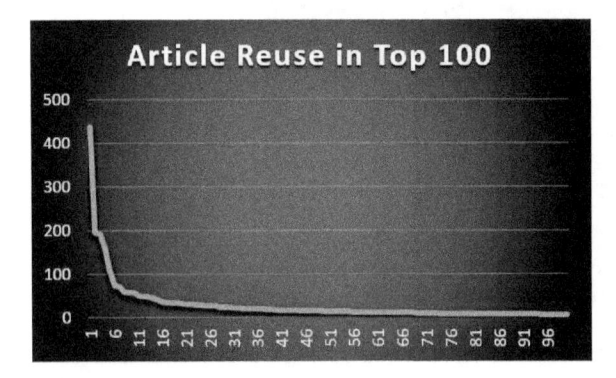

Article Reuse in Top 100

The 10 most used articles also accounted for around half of the queries (79%) and usage on the top 100 list. 10-79 relationship.

A quick analysis of these figures (with one exception, organization 1) shows that - on condition that an organization successfully identifies the ten (10) most common and requested knowledge articles - this will correspond to between 49-79% of all resolved queries on the top 100 list. Queries possible to resolve via self-service with an established and sufficiently in-depth knowledge database.

The conclusion is therefore that hundreds of knowledge articles are entirely sufficient in a self-service knowledge database, on condition the system has done a good job in identifying which articles have been requested. A further conclusion is that if we are not successful in finding a good way to identify the key articles, we risk ending up in a situation where we simply guess and write thousands of articles without any successful launch. Here, relevance is considerably more important than volume.

There are several ways to identify and choose the right articles for a launch. Set up a smaller pilot group to represent the entire organization, view new support statistics from mail or telephone support, amongst others. We should also follow and analyze the need for knowledge articles directly in the self-service tool.

One challenge - besides finding a good method for identifying the right articles for a launch - may be that there is occasionally a belief that there is need for a huge number of articles covering many different areas. Facts and statistics show that a large portion of articles in many databases are rarely or never used. When looking at the above line diagram, it is easy to understand how a few articles account for the large majority of all queries during a particular period. The requirements and the queries change constantly, which requires a process that continuously identifies the need for new articles.

The search function we use in our self-service tool enables early identification of new knowledge articles, which in turn gives us great support and a good tool to quickly identify and select the correct knowledge articles to meet the organization's needs without needing to create a vast number of knowledge articles. The old method of searching, where the user often navigated using a tree structure and hierarchy, exposes sparse content in a different way. An updated current homepage with the right articles available and a central search function in combination with a hundred (100) carefully-selected articles can go a long way and give the user a relevant self-service tool.

But with such a sparse knowledge database and only one hundred articles, it is important to have a functioning working method (read KCS).

This is dealt with in the next section of the book "How", showing you how to effectively compile the new requirements on an ongoing basis and quickly publish new articles as they are demanded. The difference is that here you really can allow demand to control production instead of guessing and making assumptions.

Outcome

Introducing a self-service portal and adapting the KCS methodology deliver tangible results within short, it fits any budget and employees experience a greater job satisfaction. It gives you the opportunity to increase the value of your customer service. Being a small company is not an argument against knowledge management. If fact, it's even more critical that you adapt a knowledge management strategy as soon as possible.

Part II – How?

Creating the future support organization that creates real customer value.

Adoption of successful self-service and Knowledge Management that embraces the shift in technology and our new behavior.

Introduction to creating the future support organization that creates real customer value

The vast majority of service desks we are consulting has experienced an increased demand for support with the same amount of support staff. Today's support teams have to deal with problems thought numerous channels. From their incident system, email, phone, chat, forums, etc. With all these channels of support available, we need to guide our customer to the correct one.

We also meet customers that are used to helping themselves. They use Google and Social Media for support, and these people are no longer eager to call the service desk with their issues. These customers want to feel empowered and self-sufficient, and achieve this by helping themselves.

The traditional service desk has a 1st, 2nd and maybe 3rd level support. As you know the more you escalate an incident, the higher the cost. But what if we can shift left? Have the support team start documenting all the knowledge they have available, and make it visible to their customer as soon as the problem occur.

This is where we introduce Level 0 support to our customers. A self-service channel where customer themselves can find the answer to their problem. We are now decreasing the support costs by organizing all knowledge in one place, and helping the customer helping themselves. Few companies have the luxury of having an always open support, but with the introduction of self-service, we are now extending our service. Suddenly we have a service channel that are open 24 hours a day, 7 days a week, all year around. A service channel that contains updated and relevant knowledge.

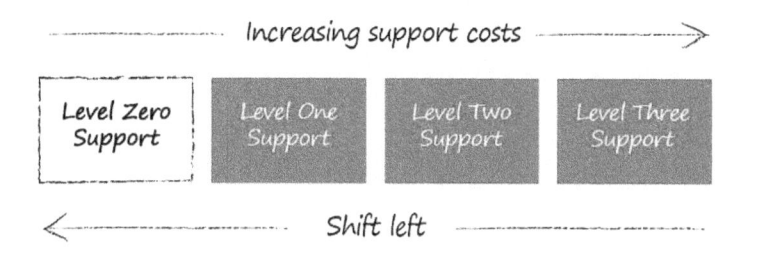

⟵ Increasing support costs ⟶

| Level Zero Support | Level One Support | Level Two Support | Level Three Support |

⟵ Shift left ⟶

So how can we guide our customer in the right direction? Make sure that they are using our service channels?
We have to emphasize and educate the people that are in daily contact with our customer. The support team.

It's the support team that have all the knowledge. It's the support team that are in daily contact with our customers. The support team tend to get a lot of negative criticism within the organization, or they are simply forgotten. But the support team are sitting on a secret treasure. They have a vast amount of knowledge. Knowledge that not only is important when supporting their customers, but for the entire organization.

Self-service reduces the number of phone calls to the service desk, it allows the service desk to spend more quality time with the customers who phones in with complex enquiries. At the same time, self-service allows the service desk to evolve into a multi-channel command center.

We have to make sure that the service desk uses the right tools and knowledge management strategies so they can perform at their best. We have to develop their personal skills, encourage team work and collaboration, as well as sharing and improving. The Consortium for Service Innovation has developed the best practice methodology Knowledge-Centered Service (KCS). The idea behind it was (and still is) that knowledge is the foundation of excellent customer service.

In contrast to traditional 'Knowledge Engineering', where knowledge is created by experts and added to a self-service channel through extensive validation processes, KCS is an integral part of daily operations within service desks. Creation and maintenance of knowledge is a natural byproduct when support agents solve customer issues.

KCS has four basic concepts:

- Create content as a by-product for solving issues
- Evolve content based on demand and usage
- Develop a self-service portal (Level 0 Support) of collective experience to date
- Reward learning, collaboration, sharing and improving.

By implementing KCS to your support organization, you will get an updated and relevant self-service channel where customer will find the answer to their questions. By making sure that your self-service portal always are up-to-date, you can easily guide your customers to the right support channel.

5 Essential Tips for self-service Success

Either you are looking to implement self-service for your customer, or assessing the quality of your current self-service solution, there are five key enablers that need to be in place in order to achieve a successful self-service solution.

Self-service is an excellent tool that we always recommend every organization to implement, as it's offering a way to save money while improving customer experience. A good self-service solution can reduce service costs, decrease incoming calls to the service desk, increase customer satisfaction as well as improving job satisfaction.

1) Findability - It does not matter how much content you have in your self-service solution if your customer can't find it. Findability is driven by context, structure, and rich environment statements. Make sure to create all content in customer's context. An easy to use template will help both structuring and writing the article, as well as making it coherent and searchable. Working with KCS (Knowledge Centred Service) enables you to create new articles as a part of your daily workflow.

You need to continuously improved content that are being used to make sure that you always have a latest information available.

2) Completeness - Your customers want to know what you know, as soon as you know it. How quickly can you have knowledge visible externally? The goal is to have most of what we know, available to self-service within 90 minutes (based on the 90/90 rule from KCS). While the 90/90 rule can seem to be a bit provoking, the primary enabler to self-service success is volume and speed. Knowledge is time sensitive, and customers expect to find answers when using self-service. A good self-service solution can solve up to ten times the amount of problems reaching level one.

3) Access – You need to make the self-service solution easily available to your customers. My recommendation is to integrate the self-service solution to the user interface.

Examples of good integrations are integrations of search results, integrated FAQ to other access points, and adding a 'was this what you where after' article solution where customers are logging their problems (solving the incident before it reaches level one). Make access to your self-service obvious and easy to find in order to engage the audience. The less effort in finding the self-service, the easier it will be to involve users.

4) Navigation – What is the number one reason for not coming back to your self-service solution? A research project done by Microsoft found that they key reason people did not come back to a self-service solution, was not that you could not find what you were looking for, but 'dead-ends'. By 'dead ends' we mean once the requestor has started interacting with your self-service, they don't have to stop and start over again if they don't find what they are looking for.

A good self-service solution should include both the ability to search for answers, and facilitate an easy-to-use browse function for all knowledge available. If your customer wants to move from the self-service solution to an assisted help solution, an integrated click-to-submit (create an incident) function or a click-to-chat function should be only one click away. Make sure that your requestors' search or browsing history is included in the request in order to minimize the transition effort. Having this solution available will make your customer be far more willing to go back and try again the next time they have a problem.

5) Marketing - Self-service requires a marketing plan. The "build it and they will come" model does not work for self-service solutions. we cannot highlight this enough for my clients. It takes time to change the behavior of your customers, but having a solid marketing plan in place will help with the transition. Get advice from those who understand how to communicate and build a marketing plan, and make sure to reinforce your plan at every opportunity available. Have a 'launch party', make coffee-mugs, have a name-the-portal competition.

Make a buzz about this splendid new self-service solution and help your customers interact with it. Other great tips like creating a pre-set message for incoming calls informing customers that they can find help in the self-service tool, are proven best-practices. If your customers like what they see, they will use it a lot!

Creating the best possible self-service solution should not be all about the work. Be creative and have fun in the process.

The process for capture, structure, reuse and improve knowledge articles

The KCS methodology consists of two loops. The A loop, The Solve Loop, represents the individual workflow that is driven by customer requests for assistance (incidents). The practices within this loop are transactional; they are what we do to resolve the customer's issue. The Solve Loop consists of Capture, Structure, Reuse and Improve.

Capture knowledge

The capture process is a procedure where we describe the process for capturing organizational need.

It is important to understand why we need to transform customer information into valuable company knowledge, as well as how to capture it in a way that makes it valuable for other to use.

Try to write down everything you know. It's impossible. Then have someone asking you questions. Suddenly you realize that you have a vast amount of knowledge. We don't know what we know until someone ask. Most of us cannot provide all information we have until we are asked the right questions.

Now applied this to your workplace. How are you creating articles for your next release? A common solution is to have premade content available at the release date. Knowledge that has been created by experts and added to a self-service channel through an extensive validation process. But how can you create the right knowledge when you don't know the questions yet? It's hard to predict what the customer is asking for, and how they are behaving toward a change until it happen.

Here are 6 guidelines to help you understand the importance of the Capture process:

Capture in the customer's context

As soon as you receive a customer request, you have to reflect over their issue. Do you understand what they are asking? It is important to understand the customer's problem prior to solving the problem. You need to write down key words and short sentences in the customer's context as whey are describing the issue. Write down complete thoughts compared to complete sentences. It is important to write down the customer's issue as soon as they describe it, in order to capture the correct concern. You wouldn't be able to remember everything once the issue is solved. This information will be the beginning of your knowledge article.

You have to have an understanding of both customer's experience and the environment surrounding it. What is the customer's need? Perception? What is the customer's experience? How is their environment? Has there been any resent changes? Use all these inputs to improve the article. Either by creating a new article with all the relevant information, or if you have discovered an existing article, add the customer's experiences in order to improve the article. It is hard to ask the questions in a way that reflects not knowing the answer once we have solved the problem. Context cannot be recreated after the fact.

Capture relevant content

If the customer's perception of the experience turn out to be wrong, it's still important to include the experience in the article. This will enhance the findability for other customers with same or similar perceptions. Do not alter the customer's perception of the problem no matter how 'wrong' you feel it is.

The 'support analyst's job is to capture with accuracy. Then, later in the process, will technical accuracy be critical for solving the problem. Technical accuracy occurs in the environment, resolution and cause.

Capture knowledge in the moment it becomes explicit

Rather than being documented after the fact, articles are created as part of the problem-solving process. There need to be a change in the organizations way of working in order to make this happen.

We need to improve the way we are working to include the article creation process. Instead of writing down everything we learn from our customer on a piece of paper, we need to start document this is a Work in Process article.

Remember to keep it short and simple, and instead of using complete sentences, use complete thoughts. It's important to start documenting the customer's issue in the right format. If we are doing articles after the incident is closed, we have missed the point and we are not doing KCS.

It's essential to ensure that we are capturing our customer's perception of the issue when they are describing the problem. Tacit information becomes explicit as the conversation takes place. Clarifying questions are important to help draw out and validate details that improve the success of problem solving.

Even if the resolution is not yet known, the problem becomes visible for other within the organization. This is especially important for others working in the same product area. This way we are not working on issues that have already been solved or are in the process of being solved.

Search as soon as you understand the issue

Searching is a form of capture. By searching your self-service channel, you greatly reduce the likelihood of working at an issue that is already solved. Search both in the customer context and by using your own key words.

Searching the self-service portal can reveal similar issues and prompt clarify questions that can validate or eliminate known issues.

Each search matters

Key search word that the customers used during the problem solving process, are recommended to be saved and analyzed. These key words can either be the beginning of new articles or metadata added to existing articles. Maybe you have to improve exiting articles in order for them to become more customer friendly.

If you can capture all the search strings the customer used in the self-service portal and make it visible to the support desk, the customer will feel that his effort searching the self-service portal was important and not a dead-end. (Never give your customer dead-ends) This information can help advance the problem-solving process as we can assess what the customer has already done. Also, since these search stings came from the customer, they are in the customer's context.

If we find a published article in the knowledge base, we should improve it to increase customer findability. If the article was a WIP or a draft, we should add everything we learned throughout our time with the customer.

Are we licensed to published the article, and have a high confidence in it (are we confident will the solution and is it compliant with the content standard?), then we should publish it to self-service.

Search words are potential new knowledge

You want both the analyst and the customers search words to be logged, as they improve or even create new knowledge articles. The customers search words are important as they are captured in the customer's context, and the analyst's search word as they contain additional information.

Capture Practice
- By-product of the problem-solving process
- Capture in customer context
- Information about the environment
- Capture knowledge when it becomes explicit
- Capture relevant content
- Understand the customer issue first
- Search the knowledgebase before you add
- Search words are candidate knowledge
- Each search matter!

Structure knowledge

"A little bit of structure goes a long way"

Now that all the knowledge has been captured, the next step is to structure it. By making sure the whole support team are following the same structure when creating new articles, we are creating knowledge in the daily work routine. By working coherently with structure, we make sure that the knowledge created is consist and user-friendly.

A common practice is to write down all the customer's information on a piece of paper that are being discarded as soon as the issue is closed. Analyst often feel that it's quicker and easier to verbally communicate the solution and the issue is never properly reported. This practice makes it harder to analyze why all the issues occurs in the first place, and what we can do to solve them faster. Another concern is the quality that is being presented to the customer.

Different analysts see and understand the issue differently, and are often giving slightly different answers. In order to give the best possible customer service, we need to be consistent in our answers every time.

Start with an easy-to-use template

Introducing KCS to the organization does not mean that everyone are turning writers overnight. KCS strive to create content that are good enough. And in order to be good enough, the content need some structure. Introducing a structured template helps with the article findability.

A good self-service tool has all the text in the article searchable. Since the article is created from the customer context, it will also be found when customers are searching for it. The knowledge base becomes findable and usable for the intended audience.

An example of an easy-to-use template is shown underneath. It is recommended to have this template represented at every agent's station, as well as regularly monitoring its usage.

Article Template

- **Issue** – (Symptom, problem & question) in customer context. What are they trying to do, or what is not working? Is this the first time this problem has occurred? Where did it occur?
- **Environment** – What products does the customer have (platform, product, release). Have there been any environmental changes? How is it configured?

- **Resolution** – (Fix & Answer) answer to the question or the steps required to solve the issue. This is often in a bullet point list with key words in bold text. Pictures is a great feature for articles that are in high demand. Even video content can enhance the quality.

- **Cause** – The underlying cause of the issue, if needed. This is often for reporting problems and defects and help the organization analyzing the matter.

- **Metadata** – Information such as article state, date created, number of times article has been used, modification history and last modified. Metadata is usually automatically generated and only key word should be added. For example, misspellings, old product names or nicknames, key words from pictures and videos if it's not in the text.

Activating Wi-Fi

Created by Administrator
10/23/15 1:01 PM

Issue
Can't ativate Wi-Fi

Environment
Nexus 5, recently updated software to version Android Lollipop 5.0.1

Resolution
After the last IOS software update, you have to manually turn on wi-fi

1. Tap **Settings**

   [Settings icon]

2. Tap Wi-Fi under **Wireless & networks**.
3. Tap the control beside **Off** to change it to **On**.

   [Wi-Fi On toggle]

What to do with Work-in-Progress knowledge articles?

After capturing all the known knowledge (often only the issue and environment at his point) in the above structure, this becomes a Work-in-Progress article. A WIP is only a temporary state and this article will either be deleted as we are detecting a current article when we continue our search, or will change state into a Draft article as we realized that we are sitting on new knowledge.

When the WIP article has been created, it is essential to search the knowledge base yet again for known articles. The reason for this is that most often, additional information has occurred from the analyst's perspective. Also, after narrowing down the problem, new information has been added and looked upon. This additional search is critical for the quality of the knowledge base.

By working this way, we reduce the problem-solving time and ensure that the new article either are creating from the need or are built on and integrated with existing knowledge.

Short and consist article that are the answer to one question

A great rule of thumb is that an article shouldn't be longer that one page, and that each article is an answer to one question. It the article is too long, it will be hard to find the solution to the customer's problem, it's easier to be confused and your customer will end up losing interest.

When looking at an online video, for example on YouTube, how long do you keep your interest up? If you realize that the video is 10 min long, how big is the chance that you will finish it? Same goes for a knowledge article. If the article comes out to long, maybe you need to edit it. Maybe the article can be divided into two or more articles. Then within the KCS practice, linking is recommend, so link between articles.

Article feedback

Article feedback is crucial to ensure the quality. If possible, the customers should be involved in the feedback process. This feedback would be in the form of rating the article, make comments and suggestions, or even having the opportunity to update the article. Getting the customer involved in the feedback process helps safeguarding a healthy and updated knowledge base.

Reuse knowledge

Do you know the amount of resource spent on resolving issues? Or the amount of rework that are taking place because knowledge is not being shared?

The reuse process makes sure that we benefits from the collective experience of the organization. We should not use our valuable time solving problems that are already being solved by a colleague. The known KCS technique *'Search early, search often'*, make sure that this will not happen.

The following techniques will help you in the KCS reuse process.

Improvement of daily work routine
Best practice for capturing information is to write down the key points in a WIP article when talking to the customer. These key points include the issue and the environment surrounding it. The next step is to search the knowledge base in real-time, guiding the customer thought the experience. A good rule is that search words and phrases are theoretically content for new articles (if one does not exists), so the search string should be saved for further analysis.

Search early, search often

The importance of searching early cannot be stressed enough. It is more time- and cost-effective to do an additional search, than starting producing a new article at an early stage. If the organization already have the solution available, use it! All early searches in the problem-solving process should be done by using all customer's information in the customer's context.

It is essential to search often as when an analyst is working on a problem, new information and additional material will occur. The analyst will then use this new information to perform an additional search using this knowledge as well has his own language. Maybe the article exists, only it is written in a difficult and complex business-language, making it next to impossible for the customer to find and understand. By learning this, the analyst can simply improve this knowledge in order to make it comprehensible for the customer.

Remember that searching is something that is done throughout the problem-solving process. It would therefore be ideal to have the search function easy available to the WIP article in order to minimize the amount of clicks. The amount of work it takes for the analyst to perform a search. If it's easily available, it will make the search process fun and motivating.

Learn from the organization's collective experience

Even if the analyst can't find an answer to the issue, similar articles will help and gain knowledge to the analyst, constructing a good foundation for the solution. This can help direct the conversation and recognize clarifying questions.

One final search to remember. The important last search before the new article is published. Other analyst may have been working on the same issue simultaneously, or producing the solution have clarified the issue even better. This last search will help with the commonly known duplication issue most organizations experience in the beginning of their KCS journey.

Referencing and linking practice

When creating knowledge articles, one can be astounded by all the information available, so always try to keep in mind that the article should be clean and simple. The pathway to the solution should be easy to find, and key word and phases should be highlighted. A great rule of thumb is to think about the article as an answer to one question, and that it should preferably not be any longer than 1-2 pages. Long, intricate articles lose the readers interest, and makes it harder to get a grip over how to solve the problem.

Are there several questions within the article? It is much better to create more articles and link between them.

This gives the customer a better view over how to solve their problem, and if interested, have the opportunity to get a more in-depth solution scenario. The organization will benefit from this practice as well. They will get a more accurate statistic over what the customer is looking for, and can make additional changes or improvement when analyzing the data.

In order to look after our knowledge and keeping our knowledge base healthy, it is highly recommended that the incident system and knowledge base are integrated. As soon as a new issue become known, and search is done, preferable within the incident tool. If the solution is found, it should be improved if needed, then linked to the incident.

The knowledge article becomes the solution, and the analyst can close the incident and move on to the next. Linking indicator is an essential element since it helps analyzing how many new vs knows issues have reached the service desk.

Data generated from the participation rate is crucial for many of the evolve loop analysis activities. Organizations that cannot associate incidents or link are at disadvantage. It will take longer for the analyst to solve each incident, and the organization will be spent more time analyzing their knowledge base.

There are 4 types of linking that can occur at the service desk:
- Linking incident to existing article
- Linking incident to non-knowledge base content
- Linking to content that can be downloaded
- Linking articles

Linking incident to existing article

After searching and finding a relevant article to the issue, the article should be read by the analyst in order to make sure it is still relevant, then the article should be linked directly to the incident. If any changes or improvement need to be done to the article, it is the analyst responsibility that this will be done. Either by the analyst himself, or if he does not have the rights to do so, flagging the article.

Linking incident to non-knowledge base content

Sometimes, in order to help the customer, there is a need to link to non-knowledge base material. This should be done cautiously. Always keep in mind the purpose of the link, and ask yourselves if it is essentially for the outcome. Furthermore, make sure to include a describable text in the article, in order to make it searchable and reusable.

Linking to content that can be downloaded
Adding attachments to an article could be very helpful, but when adding attachments there are a few questions that need to be answered in advance. Could the downloadable content be included in the article, or could it be created in a new article and link to the current one?

Who do we make sure that the customer can find the article with the attachment? Is the attachment critical for the solution? If there still is a need for an attachment, then of course, use the attachment to improve the article.

Linking articles
Linking has become a common practice and are being respected as the new standard. Today's technology encourages linking between them in order to make it easy for the users as well as collective valuable data to the organization.

For example, if you have many incidents linking to the same article, the sole problem may be the system that the article is referring to. Maybe changes or improvement is needed for this system in order to create less incidents.

Encouraging the analyst to link their incidents encourages positive participation and contribution. Then the analysts start realizing that their articles are being linked over and over again, it will boost their confidence and make creating new articles fun!

Improve knowledge

Once the KCS article creation process has started, there will be loads of articles available in the knowledge base. About 80% of these articles will never be reused. However, those remaining 20% will be used over and over again. So how do we make sure that the quality of these articles have met the company's standards? How are you going to find these articles and how is responsible for updating them?

Here are 5 recommended guidelines to help you implement and succeed when adapting the improve process:

Just in time quality

The analyst need to apply great judgement when listening to the customer. The customer will give a lot of information, and some of it will have little or no relevance to the issue. It is up to the analyst to decide what should be and shouldn't be included in the article. Could the provided information be misleading, imprecise or even inappropriate to the audience?

Is it in accordance to company policies? Is it irrelevant to this issue? A well-thought analyst knows how to capture relevant, accurate and consistent information, and how to structure it to an easy to read as well as searchable article.

When the analyst is improving existing articles, it is essential to not rewrite, edit or delete parts of the article. We always have to assure that these statements are a vital part of the article because this is how the customer perceived the issue. Always add to the problem statements.

Reuse is review

Now that we have created a great knowledge base with what we know to date, it is fundamental that we continue to update it. The goal is to create a company culture of collective ownership where everyone is in charge of their own actions. Who better to confirm the accuracy of the article than the analyst who uses it?

The analyst that uses the article is responsible for the quality in that specific article. If the analyst discover that the article need to be updated, and the analyst has the right to do so, the article should be updated before it is used as a solution. If the analyst doesn't have publishing rights, he should flag the article. This so the article can be reviewed and published by someone with publishing rights.

UFFA

UFFA stands for 'Use it, Flag it, Fix it, Add it' and is the core workflow behind the KCS concept of collaboration and collective ownership of the knowledge base.

When searching using UFFA, the analyst should:

- **Use it** – leverage and link an existing article to resolve incident
- **Flag it** – if not licensed or confident, add a comment to the article so an authorized analyst can fix it
- **Fix it** – modify an existing article if licensed and confident
- **Add it** – create a new article if one does not already exist

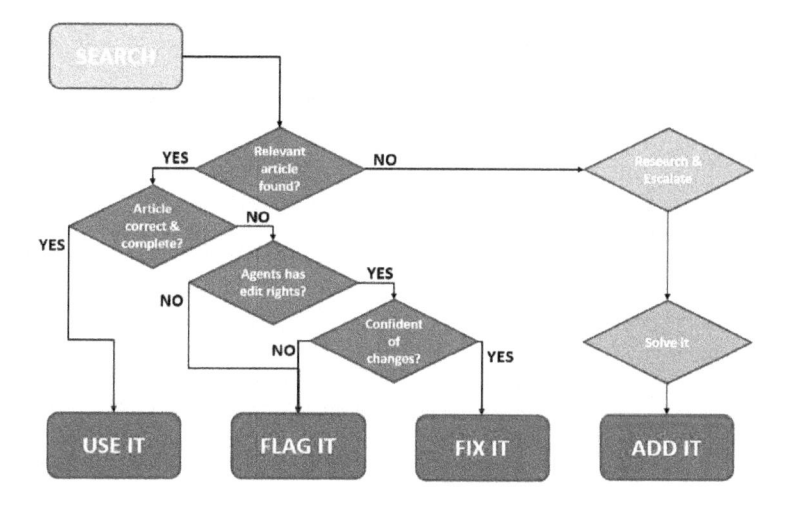

Licensed to modify

This knowledge management process ensures that important information flows freely throughout the whole organization. For organizations using KCS processes, this information is also a part of incident management and problem management processes. By storing and making available information about known issues and problems, KCS helps reduce future redundant incidents.

Analysts will have different levels of authority in the system. The proven licensing program links an analyst's rights and privileges within the system to the analyst's proven skills.

When is a new article required?

A great rule of thumb is that one article is the answer to one question.

Content health - Assessing the value of knowledge articles

Almost every organization has a large volume of content that can be configured into manuals, instructions, guides and notes. This content tends to be static with a fixed structure, rather than adaptable and easily accessible.

Today's knowledge is time-sensitive and more dynamic than ever. Information can be shared though a variety of different channels including online communities, social media, self-service, chat, email, phone calls and face-to-face conversations. Our customers are demanding an open and visible flow of information that is shared and consumed in real time. This creates a new process for how we collect, structure, reuse and improve knowledge. A mature KCS environment should be able to work by the 90/90 rule. That 90% of what you know should be visible to your customer within 90 minutes.

The solve loop flow of knowledge articles consists of content that is positioned between real-time conversations and technical manuals. This content must be sufficiently structured to work, and at the same time dynamic enough to support real-time use.

Content Continuum – the Scope of KCS

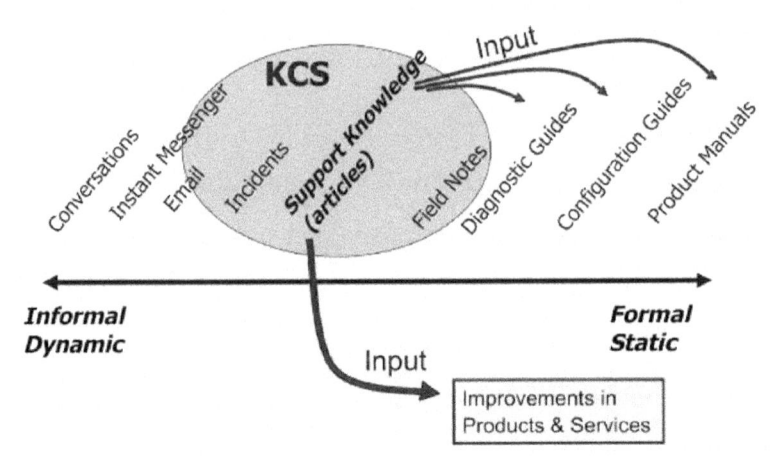

Diagram: An ellipse labeled "KCS" containing "Support Knowledge (articles)" with surrounding items along a continuum arrow from Informal/Dynamic (left) to Formal/Static (right): Conversations, Instant Messenger, Email, Incidents, Field Notes, Diagnostic Guides, Configuration Guides, Product Manuals. "Input" arrows point into KCS, and an "Input" arrow flows from KCS to a box labeled "Improvements in Products & Services".

Content health is a process in which we look at the health of our knowledge base, in other words, what value it brings to the organization and how we can improve this over time.

Here are techniques for knowledge states - Establish a standard for your knowledge.

By establishing a standard for the knowledge, we can look at the health of our knowledge base and the value it is creating for not only the service desk, but also for the whole organization over time. We need to maximize the value of what we learn in our everyday interaction.

Here are three techniques that will help with determining which audience an article should be visible to.

Article Confidence

How confident are we in the article? This technique tells us about the level of confidence we have in the content we have structured and created. All articles are worth sharing in case others are experiencing the same or similar issue. We can use the level of confidence to indicate where the article is in its life cycle. When an article has solved a problem, or has been reused, we gain confidence in its quality. As an article evolves and is reused, reviewed and enhanced, article confidence is updated.

The recommended article confidence life cycle is as follows:

Article Confidence

- Work in Progress (WIP)
- Not Validated
- Validated
- Archived

Optionally flag and move back to "Not Validated"

Work in Progress (WIP)

This article only contains an issue and environment. The resolution is not yet known, but we still want to capture what we can, and most importantly, capture it in the customer context. In complex environments where the creation of a solution can take days or longer, having WIP articles helps minimize the amount of duplicate work and promotes collaboration across the organization.

WIP may only be a temporary state. WIP articles should either become Not Validated or Validated articles, or should be disregarded (deleted) as known knowledge has been found. WIP gives us an easy way to identify and manage incomplete articles in the knowledge base.

Not Validated

The article contains an issue, environment and resolution, but the confidence in the provided resolution is low. This knowledge state helps agents capture and share their experiences since if an issue is worth answering, it is worth entering in the knowledge base. Never review all Not Validated articles, only the one that drives demand. This is a much more efficient way of producing quality knowledge.

Users with access to Not Validated articles in the knowledge base must be judicious when using these kinds of articles. If for example, you let your customers view Not Validated articles, let them know that these types of articles may help in solving their issue, however, they are to be used at their own risk. Encourage customers to provide feedback when using Not Validated articles. By letting customers provide feedback on articles, a more efficient workflow can be created.

Validated

A Validated article is considered complete and reusable. The level of confidence in the article is high, and it is compliant with the content standard. Release as many Validated article as possible to self-service.

Archived

Only when an article has no value to the knowledge base should it be archived. And only designated persons should be able to archive articles. It is much better to archive than to delete.
If an article has been linked to a request, deleting the article will result in a broken link between the knowledge base and the system of record.

Article Visibility

We need article visibility to help us in managing who gets to see what. Some articles should perhaps, only be visible internally, while others should only be visible to partners or a defined group of customers. Having rules set for article visibility in your organization will help to control what an external customer or the public has access to.

Internal – Only an internal audience within the organization has access to these articles.

Within a Domain – A group associated with, for example, a product domain, topic or department.

Partners – A trusted extension of the organization that is not an employee.

Customers – Customers or users of your product. These types of articles are usually available through a self-service channel.

Public – Anyone unidentified in the public domain. A common practice is to have these types of articles indexed and optimized for search engines like Google.

Article Governance

Article governance determines who can create and modify. There are two types of Article Governance – Experience Based and Compliance Based.

Experience Based – These types of articles are the most common and you should have as many members of the team as possible creating them.

Compliance Based - These types of articles usually represent only a small amount of all articles created. This attribute allows you to control sensitive or regulated information that requires tight control. Usually only a small group of designated people edit and improve Compliance Based articles. A common practice is to let all agents create Compliance Based WIPs to capture the customer context, then have designated small teams complete them. Everyone should be able to comment on Compliance Based articles for article improvement.

Here are 7 guidelines to help you with Content health

Avoid duplication

One of the most common causes of an unhealthy knowledge base is that you risk creating duplicates. Work on a service desk is often stressful and if an agent cannot find a knowledge article to answer a question immediately it is easy to create a duplicate.

The solution is to have a high level of discipline and always start by searching among the existing knowledge articles. There are different methods for searching for duplicates and this function is built into some knowledge tools. Another way is to identify individuals who create duplicates at an early stage by monitoring their work and key indicators, and providing them with training and explanations of how to improve their work.

Measure and improve

Since a knowledge base can contain a large volume of content and knowledge articles, it is impossible to understand the state of the database's health without making measurements. There are many indicators that can be used to view the status and most good knowledge tools measure and visualize these.

One of the key indicators is the proportion of all incidents in the case management system that link to a knowledge article with a known solution.

If this proportion is 30-40%, this indicates either a bad knowledge base or at least a knowledge base that is not used as a problem solving tool. A standard figure is 80-90%. For the service desk this means that in 80-90% of cases of all known incidents there is a complete knowledge article to use to solve the issue.

In addition to the key figure, it is necessary to validate, e.g. using solution rate of self-service, that all articles that we link to really solve the problem and are not insufficient or too general.

Allow the entire organization contribute to the improvement

Team work is key to building a healthy knowledge base and it is more important to have many contributing a little than a few individuals doing everything. The knowledge database must contain your collective knowledge, and everyone is responsible for sharing their own knowledge and for highlighting any errors they discover. There is no doubt that this is an area where one of the largest cultural changes is required, and if a feeling of teamwork and success is created, the knowledge in the database will improve, be used and create significant value for the entire organization. In this respect also, a good knowledge tool with the facility to highlight and comment will be of great assistance to awaken and enable collective responsibility.

Add customer context

Even if working practice advocates creating knowledge articles in real time when new questions and issues arise, we sometimes need to be proactive; for example, in advance of major changes in our IT environment and workplace. It may be a question of replacing old software with new software, and we know that customers/users will have a number of questions. These assumptions may be based on best practice from other organizations that have undergone the same change or from our own experiences of previous similar changes. If we work on pilot projects with smaller groups of users, these are ideal to help us find these early knowledge articles and needs. Then, when we use these in connection with support, it is even more important that we add the customers' context and listen to the words they use. This helps us improve the knowledge articles to give them customer context, it makes it easier to find in self-service and easier for users to understand. A good knowledge database has knowledge articles with customer context.

Archive old knowledge articles that are no longer used
Provided you have a good search function, it makes sense to be careful when archiving knowledge articles because the ones that are rarely requested might be very valuable when the need arises. At the same time, we do not want a knowledge database with large amounts of old and perhaps out-of-date knowledge articles taking up space and with the risk that they are displayed instead of newer articles that are more up-to-date and relevant.

Articles that have not been used for a long time in combination with a new way of working or system having been introduced can be archived. When they are archived, any links to them will still work but they will no longer be displayed in the search results for customers, only for users with high level of access in the knowledge database and who select to include the archived knowledge articles in the search result.

Even though it is difficult to generalize, one way of discovering knowledge articles that it might be time to archive is that they are rarely used in combination with a decreasing solution rate.

Structure increases value

When we work with knowledge articles, we should adhere to predefined requirements and recommendations to increase the chances of obtaining a uniform knowledge database that is familiar to customers and where they can find relevant information. Develop templates to support the work of creating knowledge articles that include relevant parts.

Common parts in a knowledge article include:
- **Issue** – Problem or question
- **Environment** – User's environment, software, hardware, etc.
- **Resolution** – Steps required to solve the problem
- **Cause** – The cause of the problem if it is known
- **Metadata** – Various data connected to the article that increase its value

Check points:
- Integrate knowledge into the regular support process
- Avoid duplication
- Measure and improve
- Allow the entire organization contribute to the improvement

- Always add customer context
- Archive old knowledge articles that are no longer used

Structure increases value.

Process integration

Process integration is the process of establishing a workflow process to support the desired approach, in which knowledge is collected, structured and shared in real time. We want to establish a process whereby knowledge in a knowledge database is not something that is created when time allows and in cycles, but is done at the same moment the need is discovered and as a natural component of the work that the service desk already does.

Process integration is about creating a natural flow between capture, structure, reuse and improve as described before, and how we support these through integration with the case management system and a knowledge management tool.

The goal is to ensure that everything is connected in a smart way and a person can create new knowledge articles at the same time as the case is recorded. It is important in this context to set up different knowledge states in the knowledge articles depending on who wrote them, how developed they are and how tested they are.

Here are 6 guidelines to help you with Process Integration

Think long-term and work on continuous improvement
The work of integrating the processes with different tools needs to be long-term. There are many good tools to support an approach with knowledge in focus and an increased ratio of self-service. The fundamental components that must be in place are a case management system and a self-service facility, where you can present knowledge articles both internally for the service desk and externally for your users or customers. You should evaluate the work on an ongoing basis and create as seamless a process as possible that you can use to capture, structure, reuse and improve knowledge in the daily support process. Nowadays there are excellent tools that go a long way to meet requirements and can be developed in order to support this way of working.

Choose a tool that supports the KCS methodology
Organizations that choose to work with Knowledge-Centered Service as a method are recommended to look at tools that support this method and ideally that are KCS verified (See http://www.thekcsacademy.net/tools/verified-tools/ for verified tools. In parallel to developing your knowledge and support process, look at the tools that are available and which features and technical benefits they offer. Suppliers and developers of knowledge tools have often developed their different tools based on experience of demand and what works best.

Do not over-modify your solution and benefit from the experience of others

It is also a major advantage if you can use a tool that you do not need to make major technical modifications to, since this often means that you can no longer benefit from the ongoing development that the system supplier carries out.

Another reason is that the benefits gained from modifying a technical tool are often outweighed by the costs in the form of testing, missed updates and bugs that do not occur in standard products.

Cloud services have many benefits - not least long-term

Increasing numbers of suppliers of tools are moving to the cloud, and today a majority of them offer a cloud service. We will not analyze all the advantages offered by cloud services here, but as cloud services have matured and usually offer a faster pace of forward development combined with ever-improving performance and accessibility, the choice of a cloud-based tool will represent a benefit, not least in the long term.

Automate and simplify

When you establish your process, the most important focus is to try to automate and simply all the different stages as much as possible.

For example, it should ideally be possible to create a draft or a "W.I.P. (work in progress)" by pressing a button directly in the case management system, where an agent has already recorded all the necessary information such as the problem, proposed solution, environment, etc.

In this case, there must be technical integration between the case management system and the knowledge tool where new knowledge articles are created.

Start work with a number of minimum requirements

Even if the process integration work must be done in stages and developed over time, there must be a number of fundamental pieces in place to enable the work to function.

We therefore recommend that, among other things, process integration and the technical solution support:

- making knowledge articles accessible for service desk and users in the form of self-service

- the ability to create new knowledge articles directly from the case management system
- a powerful and functioning search facility that comprises an important component for both service desk as well as self-service users.

Check points:
- Think long-term and work on continuous improvement
- Tool that supports the KCS method
- Do not make unnecessary modifications and benefit from the experience of others
- Cloud services provide benefits
- Automate and simplify
- Start work with a number of minimum requirements

Performance assessment

Work on improving the organization's knowledge management and achieving a better level of self-service depends on changing the mindset and building a culture where everyone works together. A culture in which everyone has common responsibility for encouraging an environment where individuals are rewarded for sharing and spreading knowledge.

Measuring the ability of an individual, the team and the whole organization to collect, structure and share knowledge is an important instrument to obtain a learning organization that discovers how to achieve positive results at an early stage and what needs to be changed for the better.

Here are 5 guidelines to help you implement process integration

Measure outcome, not activities
In a modern support organization, we want to measure real results, i.e. not to focus on activities but instead to focus on real customer value and outcome. A normal problem that most support organizations that start to introduce an approach with increased knowledge sharing and an increased level of self-service soon become aware of is that traditional metrics that are used do not support this.

The traditional support metrics are often activity-focused and measure both the wrong activities and at the wrong level. You probably want to measure a large number of key indicators to obtain a correct picture of the performance of the organization and to develop over time, but if you only measure a few key indicators, we recommend that these measure outcomes at a high level.

As long as these key indicators show positive results, you can assume that you will also deliver positive results with lower level key indicators, i.e. activities, and most importantly you create value for the organization and support your higher aims.

Two examples of good general indicators that measure outcome are:

Customer Success and Customer Satisfaction – These key indicators provide answers to whether you have satisfied customers and provide a good service.

Support cost as a percentage of total revenue - The ratio of support costs to total company revenue.

These key indicators tell you if you are providing effective support and service in relation to the business as a whole. In other words, whether a cost for providing support is reasonable at a higher level.

It can also be measured as a cost per employee. In other words, what the total support cost per employee or user is (in the case of external customer support).

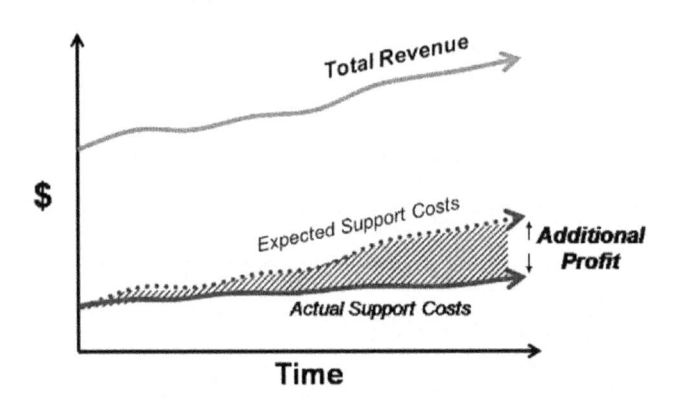

Chart showing Total Revenue, Expected Support Costs, and Actual Support Costs over Time, with the gap between Expected and Actual Support Costs labeled as Additional Profit.

When we measure key indicators, we need to understand that the more mature the self-service organization and the further we have managed to develop our approach, the more important it is that we measure the right indicators and not the traditional support indicators.

The reason for the things we have described above in the first part under "Self-service means new metrics for your support organization" is that key indicators such as: number of calls, resolution rate, time it takes to resolve the call, escalation to 2nd and 3rd line etc. are counterproductive with respect to self-service.

When an organization matures and increases the use of self-service, it means that simpler and repeated cases are mainly managed through self-service. This means that the cases that are now managed by the manned support are more complex and unique.

In turn, this leads to longer calls and lower resolution levels and probably also an increased rate of escalation to 2nd and 3rd line. The conclusion here is that if we do not introduce new key indicators that measure the usefulness of the support at a higher level for the whole organization and the activities, it looks as though we are doing a worse job than before. The reality is the opposite, because we are starting to build a functioning knowledge structure and process where users are managing to help themselves more quickly and at a lower cost as a result of our knowledge process. At the same time, we free up more time for really complex support cases that we would not otherwise have time to resolve. So, we create a higher value and need to show and measure this with the right indicators.

Roles and rights based on proven skills

The rolls must support a way of working in which everyone involved in working with the new approach at different stages and with different levels of authority can contribute as they develop their understanding and ability to support the new approach.

The roles in this knowledge work are rarely directly related to the person's role or level in the rest of the support organization but should predominantly be based on the proven skills and real results.

Even a service desk agent could have a high level of authority in the work of developing and publishing knowledge in the organization with the right qualifications, training and attitude.

Encourage teamwork

It was previously common to promote and reward our super users and specialists, and we rewarded them simply for being specialists and possessing unique knowledge. In a modern support organization, we want to encourage teamwork and cooperation, and it is important to ensure that everyone understands the value of sharing their knowledge and that the collective knowledge that we gather and structure always exceeds the value of an individual's knowledge.

The value of knowledge is realized when it is made available, and the better we are at sharing it and making that knowledge available, the higher value it has. When we work with process assessment, we must encourage behavior where the knowledge is realized and shared, and our metrics and performance indicators need to support this rather than measure the ability of individuals to, for example, resolve a telephone support case.

A person who shares knowledge in a knowledge database and self-service reaches out more widely with that knowledge and allows more people in the organization to be involved in improving and refining the knowledge to create higher value for the organization. Gamification is something which, when implemented in the right way, can promote the right behavior and approach, but also discourage team work.

Gamification must also encourage and reward behavior where the team succeeds and where individuals manage to share knowledge and create customer value instead of creating competition or focus on the activity. When building a knowledge database, gamification where we reward the team that manages to resolve support cases via self-service, for example, can be a good idea, while gamification that rewards the individual who creates the most knowledge articles can create individual thinking and a large volume of bad knowledge articles resulting in a corrupt knowledge base.

Encourage personal development

Even if the team is the most important factor, the team comprises individuals and working to create a new mindset and culture focusing on customer satisfaction and outcomes is built on individuals developing and taking responsibility.

Collectively and individually. Most people are motivated by seeing the possibility of personal development and a clear next step to work towards.

Construct a process in which everyone is working towards doing the best job and contributing towards the team, so that sooner or later they will have a higher role with more responsibility and authority.

Check points:
- Encourage the right mindset
- Encourage teamwork
- Measure outcome not activities
- Roles and rights based on proven skills
- Encourage individuals to reach the next level

Leadership and communication

Knowledge Management is mainly about people, and for that very reason work on communication and leadership has a powerful effect on everything we do, and work on knowledge and self-service in particular because it is predominantly built on cooperation and teamwork.

It is easy to see a clear relationship between organizations and leaders that have succeeded in terms of leadership and communication and the successful implementation of knowledge and self-service initiatives. At the same time, a lack of leadership and bad communication are the most common causes for certain organizations and leaders to be unsuccessful in implementing the same changes.

Communication and leadership are not easy, and it is not something that can be easily resolved with a project, instead they involve deeper things such as personality, drive, personal characteristics, experience, etc. Good leadership and proper communication can achieve a feeling of security, understanding, teamwork and, in particular, enjoyment.

One person who explains the basis for good leadership and how we build functioning teams and organizations with insight and clarity is the internationally known Simon Sinek.

We recommend that all those who want to develop their own leadership to read his inspiring books "START WITH WHY - How great leaders inspire everyone to take action", and "Leaders eat last - Why some teams pull together and others don't". There is also a large number of videos on YouTube with Simon Sinek's presentations with the same titles as his books.

Leadership

In order to be good leaders we need to understand what motivates us and makes us buy into a specific goal or plan. There are two things that motivate us more than anything else, firstly to feel "alignment to a purpose" and secondly "a sense of accomplishment and recognition".

In addition to these two aspects, which are largely about finding a feeling and a purpose, leadership is about sensitivity and, even if everyone can learn and improve their leadership, some leaders have a natural talent to enthuse and bring together a team, or an entire company, around a common goal. These are characteristics that some people have and some people don't have, and it would be wrong to try and define these differences in detail.

Therefore, a good way of increasing the chances of taking a team with you or an even larger group on a KCS initiative, is to identify these key people and natural leaders and allow them to have a prominent role. So, start by selecting your dream team.

Establish strong support from the management of the organization at an early stage

Another aspect of leadership is that all major changes in an organization must also be backed up and have strong support of the top management in the company. In a smaller company, this support must go right up to the owners at the top.

As the change is implemented, small and large obstacles will occur on the way, and when they do occur it is essential that the top management gives its full support to the initiative and the work. This anchoring should be achieved as early as possible, but it is usually easier to obtain strong support before the work has started.

The communication plan will be the map to follow

The KCS method contains a number of important and valuable building blocks, which are important for the success of the communication and leadership. Perhaps that most important building block in a KCS project is a well-developed and strong communication plan. It will be the common thread that binds the work together.

Create a Strategic Framework

The Strategic Framework links the benefits of KCS and the initiative to the goals of the organization. The Strategic Framework is also a basis for the communication plan. As described, it is important to obtain executive support, and the work of obtaining that will be a valuable way of understanding the higher purposes and goals of the work.

The strategic framework is the foundation for a successful KCS adoption and it provides context for the key stakeholders: the business, the employees, the customers, and, business partners. The framework enables us to talk with executives in business terms by correlating KCS benefits to high-level business objectives. When it comes to communication to team members the framework provides the central messaging document.

There is a lot more to read about purpose and how to create a Strategic Framework and a Communication plan in the official KCS documentation.

Reward positive examples and highlight early successes

Two simple but effective methods to create success and obtain a positive buzz in a change process are firstly to reward team members or others who set a good example and take initiative, and secondly by highlighting examples that show the work is worth doing and creates improvement.

When we reward good examples, it is important to do fairly and not promote some people and let others take a step backwards. We do not want to create an A and a B-team but a single A-team.

We want to create a secure environment with a team atmosphere and cooperation, where we take pleasure in the positive examples of others, rather than an environment where individuals step over each other in order to be seen and gain recognition.

Leaders that promote others before themselves, who stand still and show the way even if it goes against the grain, win the trust, respect and confidence of their team. Both good and bad leadership have the capacity to spread upwards and downwards in an organization.

When we have confidence in our managers and leaders, it is easier to be good leaders downwards in an organization and in our own team. If we do not have confidence from above, it often leads to worse, sometimes more micromanaged leadership, where we criticize rather than coach and support.

So, as far as possible, it is simple truth that to be a good leader it is a good start to make sure you have a good manager/leader. A leader that creates the space for you to be the best leader you can be. It works in precisely the same way as private relationships, some people make you better and have the ability to bring out our good sides, while others make us worse.

Answer WIFM for all interested parties

When introducing self-service and KCS initiative, all interested parties must understand "What's in it for me?" and it is important to answer this in the communication plan. In general, it is true that the higher up the organization or company management you are, the easier it is to buy into an approach that includes more self-service. The simple answer to this is that it depends on enabling cost savings, which all company managers appreciate.

When we look further down the organization, and perhaps specifically the service desk, it can be completely different and a simple question here could be, "Does more self-service mean that our service desk jobs are at risk?" It is not unique, but it is an important question to answer, and to explain every time a manual service is automated.

Just as with all types of change, it represents an opportunity for those who understand the new approach and find a way to contribute to this development. New approach means new opportunities.

Check points:
- Create a secure environment and trust
- Choose a good team
- Ensure strong support from the top management
- Build a culture where success is celebrated and recognized

- Use building blocks such as Strategic Framework and Communication Plan
- Communicate clearly WIFM

Marketing

How to Get your Employees to use their New Knowledge Tool with the help from marketing. Many organizations underestimate the challenges associated with the implementation and usage of a Knowledge Tool.

You have spent a numerous amount of time researching, selecting and launching a great new technology, like a cloud based Knowledge Tool, and you have been told it will revolutionize the way your organization bring together company knowledge. But how can you be certain that your employees will adopt and practice this tool, versus continuing the habit of using the traditional method that they already know?

To achieve your organizational goals, it's imperative that your employees are onboard with this investment. It all comes down to how quickly your employees are being able to adopt the new technology as well as incorporating it as a part of their daily routine.

Your job is to help your employees get comfortable with this new technology, get them to use it, and help them understand how it makes their lives better.

Here are 6 recommended strategies in order to get your employees to adopt the newly installed technology:

Select an intuitive and user-friendly product

Remember your employees' interest when looking for your new knowledge tool. Functionality is critical, but don't underestimate the user experience. Your employees should be able to have a short startup with minimal training, and the tool should be guiding your employee to the desired outcome.

Also make sure that self-help articles are easily available, and that your employees can figure out how to use it themselves. Knowledge tools that require long training programs and heavy user manuals are a certain receipt for disaster. You are looking for a tool that can enhance the daily workflow and improve the efficiency of your team in a user-friendly way.

Find key people that will become ambassadors

First of all, it's critical that you have management buy-in. If you want to succeed with your knowledge tool, you have to make sure everyone in the organization believes in it, starting at the top. Secondly, it's important that you establish a quick win early, and in order to do so, you need to find the influencers.

You want people who are able to work across the organization, have excellent communication and networking skills, as well as are most likely to adopt and be successful with the tool. Use all your resources into making these early adopters enthusiastic about the tool, as they will be your reference and internal coaches when you move forward to subsequent phase of deployment.

Make a strong communication plan

"Build it and they will come" does not work in real life. Success is something you have to work for. Even though you and your early adopters are vested in the mission, it's likely that other people within your organization are not. People have a natural preference to resist change. Work with the marketing team to develop a strong internal communication plan. Make sure to answer the "What's in it for me?" question on all levels in the organization.

Employees will see the value to both the company and themselves when receive a well-thought answer, and will in return ask to be a part of it. This is what you are after, a situation where resistance gives away to demand.

It's a journey, not a destination

Don't look at the initiatives of your new knowledge tool as a project, but rather an improved way of working. It's a journey, not a destination, and it does not have an end-date!

Employees will adapt the technology when they see the success from others using it, as well as the technology growing alongside them over time. So keep focusing on the outcome that you are trying to achieve. Are you after higher employees and customer satisfaction, or an improved employee retention? Establish baselines against with you measure progress and continue positively reinforcement.

Leveraging the knowledge tool

Motivate your employees by offering clear feedback and solutions on how to improve. Become their leader and mentor. A positive feedback is often a stronger motivator than negative one, so always recognize and reward achievement. Leverage the knowledge tool through patterns and trend analysis, and enhance the importance of team performance. Measure your team rather than individuals, and remember to set goals on outcome, not activities.

Make it Fun!

What about introduction some elements of gamification in order to make it fun and interactive. Making a thrill around your new technology can motivate and engage people much faster as rewarding behavior you want to see is more effective than penalizing behavior you don't want to see. Employees might gather points, gain financial incentives or achieve new levels of "status". Communities are encouraged as well as sharing experiences and giving feedback.

When purchasing new technology, people often attempt to lessen the risk by opposing vendors against each other and comparing coverage and complexity of features. This is only a small part of the purchasing process.

The main focus should be on assessing each vendor's ability to help the organization achieve a defined outcome. Change is difficult for all of us, and should not be taken lightly when investing in a new organizational tool. Make the most of out of your company's new knowledge tool by following these 6 steps from the beginning. By doing so, you will ensure significant return on investment and setting your entire organization up for success.

Ditches

Ditches is another name for pitfalls or other obstacles and problems. Here, we describe some common ditches that are good to be aware of and that you can prevent or completely avoid by being aware of them and planning properly.

Here are 4 common ditches

One or a few people create all knowledge articles

It is very common to have one person who has the main responsibility for processing and adding new articles to the knowledge database. It is often a person who is passionate about it and works hard to meet the demands of the business and customers for articles and self-service. The problem is that one person can make some headway but can never meet the demand for knowledge of the entire organization. Not even the best person has as much knowledge as the entire organization combined, and to increase the value of the knowledge and compile it in a knowledge database, several people in the organization need to participate and contribute.

Another problem with having a hero is that the focus on knowledge and self-service is a form of teamwork that many people in the organization need to buy into and work towards, and that feeling of teamwork cannot be created if one person is driving the work forward.

Yet another problem with a hero is that the person could leave or get sick. If that happens, in the worst case, the work would stop or at least slow down. When one person takes on the job, it is also common that other people within support and service desk do not use the knowledge database to the same extent to resolve support cases, which in turn leads to lower quality and the wrong approach.

Recommendation: Knowledge management and self-service require teamwork to function over time. Involve the right people from the start and then let it grow to include even more people.

Slice the elephant

As in all change projects, it is important not to try to create changes that are so large that they are impossible to implement.

A good setup is to start by introducing one new approach with knowledge and self-service within a specific area. This means that we learn things along the way that we can use when we subsequently scale up the project, it also means that we can show success and results before investing a lot of time and money into something.

Recommendation: Find a suitably defined area, it could be a geographical area or a specific product or service. Once the success and results have been proven, take the next step and increase the scope.

Unclear WIFM for the service-desk team and agents

It is not easy to explain why an organization, a team and an individual should invest in knowledge management and self-service. That is precisely why we have a tendency to be careless when explaining to each individual person involved why we should put the effort in. It is usually easiest to explain it to our customers, for them it means increased access to answers 24/7 and another option for them to choose from in addition to other support.

It is also relatively simple to explain to our management, because it means lower costs and an increased share of self-service, which has lower cost than manned support. However, it is more difficult to explain to our service desk teams and to individuals. The team and the individuals have to be able to see the benefit on a higher level and to understand that customers nowadays demand choice in how they receive support.

They also need to understand that it is partly a matter of changed work tasks, and with the right attitude this could represent new opportunities. If nothing changes, in the long term it usually means less satisfied customers, fewer customers and also fewer jobs. So, the team members must understand the development and the opportunity and buy in fully so they do not slow down the result or make it worse.

Recommendation: Ensure that the "What's in it for me" work is done properly for everyone affected and especially for the service desk team and the agents. Try and ensure that key people in the work are involved in explaining it and also identifying the opportunities that a different approach to work will provide.

Unclear goals, poor metrics and weak visualization Most support organizations are good at measuring activity and goals connected to the work performed by the manned support in the form of telephone calls, resolution rates, waiting times etc. However, it is common that the corresponding goals and outcomes are missing in relation to self-service and the use of articles in a knowledge database.

Many organizations are good at developing their knowledge databases and increased use in the form of self-service, without knowing about it. If we don't know about it, we don't see the full value that it creates and that means, in the long term, that there is a risk of not making necessary resources available.

Recommendation: Set clear goals for your work with knowledge and for your self-service. Use knowledge tools and technology to offer good opportunities for measurement and feedback.

Ditches summary

- One or a few people create all knowledge articles
- Slice the elephant
- Unclear WIFM for the service-desk team and agents
- Unclear goals, poor metrics and weak visualization

Glossary

Acceptance
Formal agreement that an IT Service, Process, Plan, or other Deliverable is complete, accurate, Reliable and meets its specified Requirements. Acceptance is usually preceded by Evaluation or Testing and is often required before proceeding to the next stage of a Project or Process. See Service Acceptance Criteria.

Access Management
The Process responsible for allowing Users to make use of IT Services, data, or other Assets. Access Management helps to protect the Confidentiality, Integrity and Availability of Assets by ensuring that only authorized Users are able to access or modify the Assets. Access Management is sometimes referred to as Rights Management or Identity Management.

Account Manager
A Role that is very similar to Business Relationship Manager, but includes more commercial aspects. Most commonly used when dealing with External Customers.

Accounting
The Process responsible for identifying actual Costs of delivering IT Services, comparing these with budgeted costs, and managing variance from the Budget.

Accredited
Officially authorized to carry out a Role. For example an Accredited body may be authorized to provide training or to conduct Audits.
Agreed Service Time
A synonym for Service Hours, commonly used in formal calculations of Availability. See Downtime.

Alert
A warning that a threshold has been reached, something has changed, or a Failure has occurred. Alerts are often created and managed by System Management tools and are managed by the Event Management Process.

Application
Software that provides Functions that are required by an IT Service. Each Application may be part of more than one IT Services. An Application runs on one or more Servers or Clients. See Application Management, Application Portfolio.

Application Management
The Function responsible for managing Applications throughout their Lifecycle

Application Service Provider (ASP)
An External Service Provider that provides IT Services using Applications running at the Service Provider's premises. Users access the Applications by network connections to the Service Provider.

Application Sizing
The Activity responsible for understanding the Resource Requirements needed to support a new Application, or a major Change to an existing Application. Application Sizing helps to ensure that the IT Service can meet its agreed Service Level Targets for Capacity and Performance.

Architecture
The structure of a System or IT Service, including the Relationships of Components to each other and to the environment they are in. Architecture also includes the Standards and Guidelines which guide the design and evolution of the System.

Article
A knowledge base article. This is the document that user can search for. It may be delivered via the desktop, the web, a phone, or something else. A knowledge base article is the thing that users need to solve their problems and issues.

Assessment
Inspection and analysis to check whether a Standard or set of Guidelines is being followed, that Records are accurate, or that Efficiency and Effectiveness targets are being met. See Audit.

Asset
Any Resource or Capability. Assets of a Service Provider include anything that could contribute to the delivery of a Service. Assets can be one of the following types: Management, Organization, Process, Knowledge, People, Information, Applications, Infrastructure, and Financial Capital.

Asset Management
Asset Management is the Process responsible for tracking and reporting the value and ownership of financial Assets throughout their Lifecycle. Asset Management is part of an overall Service Asset and Configuration Management Process. See Asset Register.

Attribute
A piece of information about a Configuration Item. Examples are name, location, Version number, and Cost. Attributes of CIs are recorded in the Configuration Management Database (CMDB). See Relationship.

Audit
Formal inspection and verification to check whether a Standard or set of Guidelines is being followed, that Records are accurate, or that Efficiency and Effectiveness targets are being met. An Audit may be carried out by internal or external groups. See Certification, Assessment.

Author
The role of the knowledge base article author. See Role. The author is the person responsible for writing knowledge base content. The author isn't necesarily an expert in the subject matter being written, but they have the literary skills to turn technical knowledge into easily digestible knowledge content. A knowledge base author is likely to consult extensively with a subject matter expert in order to turn "geek-speak" into language for the n00b.

Authority Matrix
Synonym for RACI.

Availability
Ability of a Configuration Item or IT Service to perform its agreed Function when required. Availability is determined by Reliability, Maintainability, Serviceability, Performance, and Security. Availability is usually calculated as a percentage. This calculation is often based on Agreed Service Time and Downtime. It is Best Practice to calculate Availability using measurements of the Business output of the IT Service.

Availability Management
The Process responsible for defining, analyzing, Planning, measuring and improving all aspects of the Availability of IT Services. Availability Management is responsible for ensuring that all IT Infrastructure, Processes, Tools, Roles etc are appropriate for the agreed Service Level Targets for Availability.

Availability Management Information System (AMIS)
A virtual repository of all Availability Management data, usually stored in multiple physical locations. See Service Knowledge Management System

Availability Plan
A Plan to ensure that existing and future Availability Requirements for IT Services can be provided Cost Effectively.

Average work time to resolve
Number of minutes consumed per incident in developing an answer, fix, bypass or workaround. Determined by dividing the total minutes worked by the number of incidents resolved

Back-out
Synonym for Remediation.

Backup
Copying data to protect against loss of Integrity or Availability of the original.

Baseline
A Benchmark used as a reference point. For example: An ITSM Baseline can be used as a starting point to measure the effect of a Service Improvement Plan A Performance Baseline can be used to measure changes in Performance over the lifetime of an IT Service A Configuration Management Baseline can be used to enable the IT Infrastructure to be restored to a known Configuration if a Change or Release fails

Best Practice
Proven Activities or Processes that have been successfully used by multiple Organizations. ITIL is an example of Best Practice. Structuring your helpdesk/service desk on the principles of delivering relevant, contextual knowledge is best practice. People want answers.

Brain
According to KCS - "The KB does not replace people's brains; it complements their brains. People have to be able to recognize a correct answer when they see it. A user should never deliver/apply an Article they do not know enough about. They must have some level of certainty that it fixes the problem."

Business Capacity Management (BCM)
In the context of ITSM, Business Capacity Management is the Activity responsible for understanding future Business Requirements for use in the Capacity Plan. See Service Capacity Management.

Business Case
Justification for a significant item of expenditure. Includes information about Costs, benefits, options, issues, Risks, and possible problems. See Cost Benefit Analysis.

Business Continuity Management (BCM)
The Business Process responsible for managing Risks that could seriously impact the Business. BCM safeguards the interests of key stakeholders, reputation, brand and value creating activities. The BCM Process involves reducing Risks to an acceptable level and planning for the recovery of Business Processes should a disruption to the Business occur. BCM sets the Objectives, Scope and Requirements for IT Service Continuity Management.

Business Continuity Plan (BCP)
A Plan defining the steps required to Restore Business Processes following a disruption. The Plan will also identify the triggers for Invocation, people to be involved, communications etc. IT Service Continuity Plans form a significant part of Business Continuity Plans.

Business Impact Analysis (BIA)
BIA is the Activity in Business Continuity Management that identifies Vital Business Functions and their dependencies. These dependencies may include Suppliers, people, other Business Processes, IT Services etc. BIA defines the recovery requirements for IT Services. These requirements include Recovery Time Objectives, Recovery Point Objectives and minimum Service Level Targets for each IT Service.

Business Relationship Manager (BRM)
A Role responsible for maintaining the Relationship with one or more Customers. This Role is often combined with the Service Level Manager Role. See Account Manager.

Business Unit
A segment of the Business which has its own Plans, Metrics, income and Costs. Each Business Unit owns Assets and uses these to create value for Customers in the form of goods and Services.

Call deflection
The number of customer issues solved through self-service that would have become incidents (this is a subset of self-service customer success)

Capability
The ability of an Organization, person, Process, Application, Configuration Item or IT Service to carry out an Activity. Capabilities are intangible Assets of an Organization. See Resource.

Capability Maturity Model (CMM)
The Capability Maturity Model for Software (also known as the CMM and SW-CMM) is a model used to identify Best Practices to help increase Process Maturity. CMM was developed at the Software Engineering Institute (SEI) of Carnegie Mellon University. In 2000, the SW-CMM was upgraded to CMMI® (Capability Maturity Model Integration). The SEI no longer maintains the SW-CMM model, its associated appraisal methods, or training materials.

Capacity
The maximum Throughput that a Configuration Item or IT Service can deliver whilst meeting agreed Service Level Targets. For some types of CI, Capacity may be the size or volume, for example a disk drive.

Capacity Management
The Process responsible for ensuring that the Capacity of IT Services and the IT Infrastructure is able to deliver agreed Service Level Targets in a Cost Effective and timely manner. Capacity Management considers all Resources required to deliver the IT Service, and plans for short,

Capacity Management Information System (CMIS)
A virtual repository of all Capacity Management data, usually stored in multiple physical locations. See Service Knowledge Management System.

Capacity Plan
A Capacity Plan is used to manage the Resources required to deliver IT Services. The Plan contains scenarios for different predictions of Business demand, and costed options to deliver the agreed Service Level Targets.

Capture
The process and stage by which a helpdesk or service desk operator understands and documents the isses that a client/customer may have. Capturing data is what helpdesk is all about. Whether it comes via phone, fax, email, Twitter, Facebook or whatever, capturing the customer experience is vital to the Knowledge-Centered Service methodology.

Category
A named group of things that have something in common. Categories are used to group similar things together. For example Cost Types are used to group similar types of Cost. Incident Categories are used to group similar types of Incident, CI Types are used to group similar types of Configuration Item.

Cause
A section within a knowledge base article that explains why an issue has arisen. A "cause" may also be a code within service management software that is entered at the point of job/ticket resolution.

Certification
Issuing a certificate to confirm Compliance to a Standard. Certification includes a formal Audit by an independent and Accredited body. The term Certification is also used to mean awarding a certificate to verify that a person has achieved a qualification.

Certified
Did you know you and your organization can become KCS certified?

Change
The addition, modification or removal of anything that could have an effect on IT Services. The Scope should include all IT Services, Configuration Items, Processes, Documentation etc.

Change Advisory Board (CAB)
A group of people that advises the Change Manager in the Assessment, prioritisation and scheduling of Changes. This board is usually made up of representatives from all areas within the IT Service Provider, the Business, and Third Parties such as Suppliers

Change Management
The Process responsible for controlling the Lifecycle of all Changes. The primary objective of Change Management is to enable beneficial Changes to be made, with minimum disruption to IT Services.

Change Model
A repeatable way of dealing with a particular Category of Change. A Change Model defines specific pre-defined steps that will be followed for a Change of this Category. Change Models may be very simple, with no requirement for approval (e.g. Password Reset) or may be very complex with many steps that require approval (e.g. major software Release). See Standard Change, Change Advisory Board

Change Record
A Record containing the details of a Change. Each Change Record documents the Lifecycle of a single Change. A Change Record is created for every Request for Change that is received, even those that are subsequently rejected. Change Records should reference the Configuration Items that are affected by the Change. Change Records are stored in the Configuration Management System.

Change Request
Synonym for Request for Change.

Change Schedule
A Document that lists all approved Changes and their planned implementation dates. A Change Schedule is sometimes called a Forward Schedule of Change, even though it also contains information about Changes that have already been implemented.

CI Type
A Category that is used to Classify CIs. The CI Type identifies the required Attributes and Relationships for a Configuration Record. Common CI Types include: hardware, Document, User etc.

Classification
The act of assigning a Category to something. Classification is used to ensure consistent management and reporting. CIs, Incidents, Problems, Changes etc. are usually classified.
Classification Also
The process by which knowledge is organized. Each knowledge base article is classified according to it's purpose, intended audience, technical level, content etc. Classification plays an important part in how knowledge articles are searched, found and rated.

COBIT
Control Objectives for Information and related Technology (COBIT) provides guidance and Best Practice for the management of IT Processes. COBIT is published by the IT Governance Institute. See http://www.isaca.org/ for more information.

Collaboration
Creating a culture of knowledge is a team effort. Unify your management, helpdesk staff, technical geeks and others to make it work.

Competency profile
Percentage of analysts at each level of the KCS competencies

Compliance
Ensuring that a Standard or set of Guidelines is followed, or that proper, consistent accounting or other practices are being employed.

Component CI
A Configuration Item that is part of an Assembly. For example, a CPU or Memory CI may be part of a Server CI.

Confidentiality
A security principle that requires that data should only be accessed by authorized people.

Configuration
A generic term, used to describe a group of Configuration Items that work together to deliver an IT Service, or a recognizable part of an IT Service. Configuration is also used to describe the parameter settings for one or more CIs.

Configuration Baseline
A Baseline of a Configuration that has been formally agreed and is managed through the Change Management process. A Configuration Baseline is used as a basis for future Builds, Releases and Changes.

Configuration Control
The Activity responsible for ensuring that adding, modifying or removing a CI is properly managed, for example by submitting a Request for Change or Service Request.

Configuration Item (CI)

Any Component that needs to be managed in order to deliver an IT Service. Information about each CI is recorded in a Configuration Record within the Configuration Management System and is maintained throughout its Lifecycle by Configuration Management. CIs are under the control of Change Management. CIs typically include IT Services, hardware, software, buildings, people, and formal documentation such as Process documentation and SLAs.

Configuration Management

The Process responsible for maintaining information about Configuration Items required to deliver an IT Service, including their Relationships. This information is managed throughout the Lifecycle of the CI. Configuration Management is part of an overall Service Asset and Configuration Management Process.

Configuration Management Database (CMDB)

A database used to store Configuration Records throughout their Lifecycle. The Configuration Management System maintains one or more CMDBs, and each CMDB stores Attributes of CIs, and Relationships with other CIs.

Configuration Management System (CMS)

A set of tools and databases that are used to manage an IT Service Provider's Configuration data. The CMS also includes information about Incidents, Problems, Known Errors, Changes and Releases; and may contain data about employees, Suppliers, locations, Business Units, Customers and Users. The CMS includes tools for collecting, storing, managing, updating, and presenting data about all Configuration Items and their Relationships. The CMS is maintained by Configuration Management and is used by all IT Service Management Processes. See Configuration Management Database, Service Knowledge Management System.

Consortium for service innovation (CSI)

Custodians of KCS www.serviceinnovation.org

Continual Service Improvement (CSI)
A stage in the Lifecycle of an IT Service and the title of one of the Core ITIL publications. Continual Service Improvement is responsible for managing improvements to IT Service Management Processes and IT Services. The Performance of the IT Service Provider is continually measured and improvements are made to Processes, IT Services and IT Infrastructure in order to increase Efficiency, Effectiveness, and Cost Effectiveness. See Plan-Do-Check-Act.

Control Processes - The ISO/IEC 20000
Process group that includes Change Management and Configuration Management.

Cost Benefit Analysis
An Activity that analyses and compares the Costs and the benefits involved in one or more alternative courses of action. See Business Case, Net Present Value, Internal Rate of Return, Return on Investment, Value on Investment.

Cost per incident
Total support costs divided by the number of incidents closed

Critical Success Factor (CSF)
Something that must happen if a Process, Project, Plan, or IT Service is to succeed. KPIs are used to measure the achievement of each CSF. For example a CSF of "protect IT Services when making Changes" could be measured by KPIs such as "percentage reduction of unsuccessful Changes", "percentage reduction in Changes causing Incidents" etc.
Cross-functional measures
Measures to which multiple functions within the organization contribute. For example, product improvements require support to capture the interactions and recognize trends to give development credible input on high leverage opportunities for product improvement. Development must execute on these opportunities. The measure is shared by support and development.

Cultural health
Support analysts' attitude with respect to trust, commitment, conflict resolution, accountability, and focus on results.

Customer
Someone who buys goods or Services. The Customer of an IT Service Provider is the person or group who defines and agrees the Service Level Targets. The term Customers is also sometimes informally used to mean Users, for example "this is a Customer focussed Organization".

Customer loyalty
The level of emotional connection a customer feels towards the company, a longer-term measure of overall relationship. Indicators include renewal rate, new product/upgrade adoption rate, and reference ability

Customer satisfaction
Transaction-based measure of the degree to which we have met the customer expectations. This is a short-term measure of the customer experience with support. Indicators are speed or average work time to resolve, "percentage first contact resolution", technical knowledge, and politeness of the support analyst

Dashboard
A graphical representation of overall IT Service Performance and Availability. Dashboard images may be updated in real-time, and can also be included in management reports and web pages. Dashboards can be used to support Service Level Management, Event Management or Incident Diagnosis.

Database
The storage mechanism that keeps all of your data and knowledge. Most ITSM software stores its information in a database system.

Data-toInformation-toKnowledge-toWisdom (DIKW)
A way of understanding the relationships between data, information, knowledge, and wisdom. DIKW shows how each of these builds on the others.

Definitive Media Library (DML)
One or more locations in which the definitive and approved versions of all software Configuration Items are securely stored. The DML may also contain associated CIs such as licenses and documentation. The DML is a single logical storage area even if there are multiple locations. All software in the DML is under the control of Change and Release Management and is recorded in the Configuration Management System. Only software from the DML is acceptable for use in a Release.

Demand Management
Activities that understand and influence Customer demand for Services and the provision of Capacity to meet these demands. At a Strategic level Demand Management can involve analysis of Patterns of Business Activity and User Profiles. At a Tactical level it can involve use of Differential Charging to encourage Customers to use IT Services at less busy times. See Capacity Management.

Deming Cycle
Synonym for Plan Do Check Act.

Detection
"A stage in the Incident Lifecycle. Detection results in the Incident becoming known to the Service Provider. Detection can be automatic, or can be the result of a User logging an Incident."

Differential Charging
A technique used to support Demand Management by charging different amounts for the same IT Service Function at different times.

Direct Cost
A cost of providing an IT Service which can be allocated in full to a specific Customer, Cost Centre, Project etc. For example cost of providing non-shared servers or software licenses. See Indirect Cost.

Directory Service
An Application that manages information about IT Infrastructure available on a network, and corresponding User access Rights.

Domain
The field of expertise in a subject matter. If you are an expert, or know something about something, then you are an expert in that "domain". Domain experts should be consulted as part of the knowledge base creation process. Domain experts know the subject, but they don't necessarily know how to write. This is where the "Author" comes in.

Double loop
The process by which knowledge is delivered via a solve loop, and an evolve loop. Knowledge articles are created to solve a problem, and then evolve over time (or are retired) as required.

Downtime
The time when a Configuration Item or IT Service is not Available during its Agreed Service Time. The Availability of an IT Service is often calculated from Agreed Service Time and Downtime.

Effectiveness
A measure of whether the Objectives of a Process, Service or Activity have been achieved. An Effective Process or Activity is one that achieves its agreed Objectives. See KPI.

Efficiency
A measure of whether the right amount of resources have been used to deliver a Process, Service or Activity. An Efficient Process achieves its Objectives with the minimum amount of time, money, people or other resources. See KPI.

Efficiency
When you provide answers to your staff and clients, and foster an environment of knowledge creation, sharing and education, you realize this.

Email
The source of many KCS-related operations. People email the helpdesk or service desk. They want answers!

Emergency Change
A Change that must be introduced as soon as possible. For example to resolve a Major Incident or implement a Security patch. The Change Management Process will normally have a specific Procedure for handling Emergency Changes. See Emergency Change Advisory Board (ECAB).

Emergency Change Advisory Board (ECAB)
A sub-set of the Change Advisory Board who make decisions about high impact Emergency Changes. Membership of the ECAB may be decided at the time a meeting is called, and depends on the nature of the Emergency Change.

Employee loyalty
The level of emotional connection employees feel towards the company, gauged through surveys or in the cultural baseline.

Employee turnover rate
Internal and external attrition, the rate at which support analysts are leaving the support organization

Environment
Associated with information within a knowledge base article. Refers to the products involved (hardware, software, and networks) release or version, recent changes to the environment. Gives context to searches, platforms and the users' experience.

Error
A design flaw or malfunction that causes a Failure of one or more Configuration Items or IT Services. A mistake made by a person or a faulty Process that impacts a CI or IT Service is also an Error.

Escalation
An Activity that obtains additional Resources when these are needed to meet Service Level Targets or Customer expectations. Escalation may be needed within any IT Service Management Process, but is most commonly associated with Incident Management, Problem Management and the management of Customer complaints. There are two types of Escalation, Functional Escalation and Hierarchic Escalation.

Event
A change of state which has significance for the management of a Configuration Item or IT Service. The term Event is also used to mean an Alert or notification created by any IT Service, Configuration Item or Monitoring tool. Events typically require IT Operations personnel to take actions, and often lead to Incidents being logged.

Event Management
The Process responsible for managing Events throughout their Lifecycle. Event Management is one of the main Activities of IT Operations.

Evolve loop
Knowledge content evolves over time according to relevancy, feedback and technical changes. Different people with different skills assume roles to foster a continuous improvement process of knowledge content.

Exception Report
A Document containing details of one or more KPIs or other important targets that have exceeded defined Thresholds.

External Service Provider
An IT Service Provider which is part of a different Organization to their Customer. An IT Service Provider may have both Internal Customers and External Customers. See Type III Service Provider.

Facilities Management
The Function responsible for managing the physical Environment where the IT Infrastructure is located. Facilities Management includes all aspects of managing the physical Environment, for example power and cooling, building Access Management, and environmental Monitoring.

FAQ
"Frequently asked question" - A style of knowledge article that "asks" the question, then answers it.

Fault Tree Analysis (FTA)
A technique that can be used to determine the chain of Events that leads to a Problem. Fault Tree Analysis represents a chain of Events using Boolean notation in a diagram.

Feedback
Feedback is vital in effective KCS. Articles are improved over time due to feedback from clients, customers, colleagues, and anyone else who reads and consumes a knowledge article. Make sure you take the time to notice and take action based on your feedback. See Evolve loop

Financial Management
The Function and Processes responsible for managing an IT Service Provider's Budgeting, Accounting and Charging Requirements.

Fishbone Diagram
Synonym for Ishikawa Diagram.

Fit for Purpose
An informal term used to describe a Process, Configuration Item, IT Service etc. that is capable of meeting its Objectives or Service Levels. Being Fit for Purpose requires suitable Design, implementation, Control and maintenance.

Fix
A knowledge base article may refer to a "fix". This is the process/solution that will fix the issue experiences by the user.

Fixed Cost
A Cost that does not vary with IT Service usage. For example the cost of Server hardware. See Variable Cost.

Follow the Sun
A methodology for using service desks and Support Groups around the world to provide seamless 24 * 7 Service. Calls, Incidents, Problems and Service Requests are passed between groups in different time zones.

Function
A team or group of people and the tools they use to carry out one or more Processes or Activities. For example the service desk. The term Function also has two other meanings ⅜ An intended purpose of a Configuration Item, Person, Team, Process, or IT Service. For example one Function of an Email Service may be to store and forward outgoing mails, one Function of a Business Process may be to dispatch goods to Customers. ⅜ To perform the intended purpose correctly, "The computer is Functioning"

Gap Analysis
An Activity which compares two sets of data and identifies the differences. Gap Analysis is commonly used to compare a set of Requirements with actual delivery. See Benchmarking.

Governance
Ensuring that Policies and Strategy are actually implemented, and that required Processes are correctly followed. Governance includes defining Roles and responsibilities, measuring and reporting, and taking actions to resolve any issues identified.

Help
KCS is perfect for client self-service. If you have a web-based self-service platform, the principles of Knowledge-Centered Service are perfect. Clients help themselves.

Hierarchic Escalation
Informing or involving more senior levels of management to assist in an Escalation.

Impact
A measure of the effect of an Incident, Problem or Change on Business Processes. Impact is often based on how Service Levels will be affected. Impact and Urgency are used to assign Priority.

Improvement
This is a key principle of KCS. Whatever you have written...improve it. As environment, users and technical details change, update your content to keep it relevant.

Incident
An unplanned interruption to an IT Service or a reduction in the Quality of an IT Service. Failure of a Configuration Item that has not yet impacted Service is also an Incident. For example Failure of one disk from a mirror set.

Incident Management
The Process responsible for managing the Lifecycle of all Incidents. The primary Objective of Incident Management is to return the IT Service to Users as quickly as possible.

Incident Record
A Record containing the details of an Incident. Each Incident record documents the Lifecycle of a single Incident.

Incident volume
Number of incidents, cases, or tickets opened

Incomplete articles
Refers to knowledge base articles that are a work-in-progress. Role-based knowledge creation is a central theme in Knowledge-Centered Service.

Indirect Cost
A Cost of providing an IT Service which cannot be allocated in full to a specific Customer. For example Cost of providing shared Servers or software licenses. Also known as Overhead. See Direct Cost.

Information Security Management (ISM)
The Process that ensures the Confidentiality, Integrity and Availability of an Organization's Assets, information, data and IT Services.

Information Security Management System (ISMS)
The framework of Policy, Processes, Standards, Guidelines and tools that ensures an Organization can achieve its Information Security Management Objectives.

Information Security Policy
The Policy that governs the Organization's approach to Information Security Management.

Information Technology (IT)
The use of technology for the storage, communication or processing of information. The technology typically includes computers, telecommunications, Applications and other software. The information may include Business data, voice, images, video, etc. Information Technology is often used to support Business Processes through IT Services.

Integrity
A security principle that ensures data and Configuration Items are only modified by authorized personnel and Activities. Integrity considers all possible causes of modification, including software and hardware Failure, environmental Events, and human intervention.

Internal Service Provider
An IT Service Provider which is part of the same Organization as their Customer. An IT Service Provider may have both Internal Customers and External Customers. See Type I Service Provider, Type II Service Provider, Insource.

International Organization for Standardization (ISO)
The International Organization for Standardization (ISO) is the world's largest developer of Standards. ISO is a non-governmental organization which is a network of the national standards institutes of 156 countries. Further information about ISO is available from http://www.iso.org/

Ishikawa Diagram
A technique that helps a team to identify all the possible causes of a Problem. Originally devised by Kaoru Ishikawa, the output of this technique is a diagram that looks like a fishbone.

ISO 9000
A generic term that refers to a number of international Standards and Guidelines for Quality Management Systems. See http://www.iso.org/ for more information. See ISO.

ISO 9001
An international Standard for Quality Management Systems. See ISO 9000, Standard.

ISO/IEC 17799
ISO Code of Practice for Information Security Management. See Standard.

ISO/IEC 20000
ISO Specification and Code of Practice for IT Service Management. ISO/IEC 20000 is aligned with ITIL Best Practice.

ISO/IEC 27001
ISO Specification for Information Security Management. The corresponding Code of Practice is ISO/IEC 17799. See Standard.

IT Infrastructure
All of the hardware, software, networks, facilities etc. that are required to Develop, Test, deliver, Monitor, Control or support IT Services. The term IT Infrastructure includes all of the Information Technology but not the associated people, Processes and documentation.

IT Operations
Activities carried out by IT Operations Control, including Console Management, Job Scheduling, Backup and Restore, and Print and Output Management. IT Operations is also used as a synonym for Service Operation.

IT Operations Control
The Function responsible for Monitoring and Control of the IT Services and IT Infrastructure. See Operations Bridge.

IT Operations Management
The Function within an IT Service Provider which performs the daily Activities needed to manage IT Services and the supporting IT Infrastructure. IT Operations Management includes IT Operations Control and Facilities Management.

IT Service
A Service provided to one or more Customers by an IT Service Provider. An IT Service is based on the use of Information Technology and supports the Customer's Business Processes. An IT Service is made up from a combination of people, Processes and technology and should be defined in a Service Level Agreement.

IT Service Continuity Management (ITSCM)
The Process responsible for managing Risks that could seriously impact IT Services. ITSCM ensures that the IT Service Provider can always provide minimum agreed Service Levels, by reducing the Risk to an acceptable level and Planning for the Recovery of IT Services. ITSCM should be designed to support Business Continuity Management.

IT Service Continuity Plan
A Plan defining the steps required to Recover one or more IT Services. The Plan will also identify the triggers for Invocation, people to be involved, communications etc. The IT Service Continuity Plan should be part of a Business Continuity Plan.

IT Service Management (ITSM)
The implementation and management of Quality IT Services that meet the needs of the Business. IT Service Management is performed by IT Service Providers through an appropriate mix of people, Process and Information Technology. See Service Management.

IT Service Management Forum (itSMF)
The IT Service Management Forum is an independent Organization dedicated to promoting a professional approach to IT Service Management. The itSMF is a not-for-profit membership Organization with representation in many countries around the world (itSMF Chapters). The itSMF and its membership contribute to the development of ITIL and associated IT Service Management Standards. See http://www.itsmf.com/ for more information.

ITIL
A set of Best Practice guidance for IT Service Management. ITIL is owned by the OGC and consists of a series of publications giving guidance on the provision of Quality IT Services, and on the Processes and facilities needed to support them. See http://www.itil.co.uk/ for more information.

Journey
KCS and self-service is a journey. It takes time to adopt, to train, to embrace it. Getting the organization to collaborate, share and improve articles may take a significant cultural shift. Enjoy the journey - it's worth it.

Just in time ...or JIT
The concept that information is available in real time. You have a problem....I have the solution (and I'll write it in a knowledge base article). If an article doesn't exist, start work on it right there and then.

Kepner & Tregoe Analysis
A structured approach to Problem solving. The Problem is analysed in terms of what, where, when and extent. Possible causes are identified. The most probable cause is tested. The true cause is verified.

Key Performance Indicator (KPI)
A Metric that is used to help manage a Process, IT Service or Activity. Many Metrics may be measured, but only the most important of these are defined as KPIs and used to actively manage and report on the Process, IT Service or Activity. KPIs should be selected to ensure that Efficiency, Effectiveness, and Cost Effectiveness are all managed. See Critical Success Factor.

Knowledge Base
A logical database containing the data used by the Service Knowledge Management System.

Knowledge Management
The Process responsible for gathering, analyzing, storing and sharing knowledge and information within an Organization. The primary purpose of Knowledge Management is to improve Efficiency by reducing the need to rediscover knowledge. See Data-to-Information-to-Knowledge-to-Wisdom, Service Knowledge Management System.

Known Error
A Problem that has a documented Root Cause and a Workaround. Known Errors are created and managed throughout their Lifecycle by Problem Management. Known Errors may also be identified by Development or Suppliers.

Known Error Database (KEDB)
A database containing all Known Error Records. This database is created by Problem Management and used by Incident and Problem Management. The Known Error Database is part of the Service Knowledge Management System.

Known Error Record
A Record containing the details of a Known Error. Each Known Error Record documents the Lifecycle of a Known Error, including the Status, Root Cause and Workaround. In some implementations a Known Error is documented using additional fields in a Problem Record.

Known issue
An issue, helpdesk request, or service management problem that has already been documented, resolved and closed. Knowledge base articles can be created for the benefit of other clients/customer who experience the effects of the known issue.

Lifecycle
The various stages in the life of an IT Service, Configuration Item, Incident, Problem, Change etc. The Lifecycle defines the Categories for Status and the Status transitions that are permitted. For example: The Lifecycle of an Application includes Requirements, Design, Build, Deploy, Operate, Optimise. The Expanded Incident Lifecycle includes Detect, Respond, Diagnose, Repair, Recover, Restore. The lifecycle of a Server may include: Ordered, Received, In Test, Live, Disposed etc.

Linking
Once a knowledge article has been created, link it to other knowledge content. This may include other articles, incidents, problems, websites, other documents etc.

Listen
Listen to the way people express their problem, their issue and their concerns. Use this language when you author knowledge articles. People will search for words in the manner in which they speak. Use synoymns in your article, or in additonal searchable fields.

Maintainability
A measure of how quickly and Effectively a Configuration Item or IT Service can be restored to normal working after a Failure. Maintainability is often measured and reported as MTRS. Maintainability is also used in the context of Software or IT Service Development to mean ability to be Changed or Repaired easily.

Major Incident
The highest Category of Impact for an Incident. A Major Incident results in significant disruption to the Business.

Management of Risk (MoR)
The OGC methodology for managing Risks. MoR includes all the Activities required to identify and Control the exposure to Risk which may have an impact on the achievement of an Organization's Business Objectives. See http://www.m-o-r.org/ for more details.

Manual Workaround
A Workaround that requires manual intervention. Manual Workaround is also used as the name of a Recovery Option in which The Business Process Operates without the use of IT Services. This is a temporary measure and is usually combined with another Recovery Option.

Maturity Level
A named level in a Maturity model such as the Carnegie Mellon Capability Maturity Model Integration.

Mean Time Between Failures (MTBF)
A Metric for measuring and reporting Reliability. MTBF is the average time that a Configuration Item or IT Service can perform its agreed Function without interruption. This is measured from when the CI or IT Service starts working, until it next fails.

Mean Time Between Service Incidents (MTBSI)
A Metric used for measuring and reporting Reliability. MTBSI is the mean time from when a System or IT Service fails, until it next fails. MTBSI is equal to MTBF + MTRS.

Mean Time To Repair (MTTR)
The average time taken to repair a Configuration Item or IT Service after a Failure. MTTR is measured from when the CI or IT Service fails until it is Repaired. MTTR does not include the time required to Recover or Restore. MTTR is sometimes incorrectly used to mean Mean Time to Restore Service.

Mean Time to Restore Service (MTRS)
The average time taken to Restore a Configuration Item or IT Service after a Failure. MTRS is measured from when the CI or IT Service fails until it is fully Restored and delivering its normal functionality. See Maintainability, Mean Time to Repair.

Meta data
The "other" information that compliments a knowledge article. "Meta"=Greek for "around". Data like "date created", "created by", "last updated by", "date last updated", "Rating"....etc. This is important information - data that "surrounds" your knowledge.

Methodology
A structure approach. KCS is a process, an approach, a methodology. A way of making knowledge work harder in your organization. It takes committment, discipline, structure education and persistence....like any methodology.

Metric
Something that is measured and reported to help manage a Process, IT Service or Activity. See KPI.

Mission Statement
The Mission Statement of an Organization is a short but complete description of the overall purpose and intentions of that Organization. It states what is to be achieved, but not how this should be done.

Moderator
A role within the KCS process. When customers, staff or others rate knowledge base content, they may leave comments and feedback. The role of the moderator is to determine whether that feedback should be make public so that other people can see it. A moderator may decide to remove the knowledge base article from public attention based on feedback.

Monitor
Keep an eye on your knowledge processes. Define roles and assign responsibility to people so that they check and refine knowledge base content. See Feedback.

Notional Charging
An approach to Charging for IT Services. Charges to Customers are calculated and Customers are informed of the charge, but no money is actually transferred. Notional Charging is sometimes introduced to ensure that Customers are aware of the Costs they incur, or as a stage during the introduction of real Charging.

Office of Government Commerce (OGC)
OGC owns the ITIL brand (copyright and trademark). OGC is a UK Government department that supports the delivery of the government's procurement agenda through its work in collaborative procurement and in raising levels of procurement skills and capability with departments. It also provides support for complex public sector projects.

Operational Level Agreement (OLA)
An Agreement between an IT Service Provider and another part of the same Organization. An OLA supports the IT Service Provider's delivery of IT Services to Customers. The OLA defines the goods or Services to be provided and the responsibilities of both parties. For example there could be an OLA $\frac{35}{17}$ between the IT Service Provider and a procurement department to obtain hardware in agreed times $\frac{35}{17}$ between the service desk and a Support Group to provide Incident Resolution in agreed times. See Service Level Agreement.

Opinion
Embrace feedback! Give your clients a say- they have opinions! When you create knowledge base articles for public consumption, be prepared to accept, acknolwedge and act on the feedback that comes your way. Client feedback and rating is a key part of KCS principles.

Outsourcing
Using an External Service Provider to manage IT Services. See Service Sourcing, Type III Service Provider.

Overhead
Synonym for Indirect cost

Pain Value Analysis
A technique used to help identify the Business Impact of one or more Problems. A formula is used to calculate Pain Value based on the number of Users affected, the duration of the Downtime, the Impact on each User, and the cost to the Business (if known).

Pareto Principle
A technique used to prioritise Activities. The Pareto Principle says that 80% of the value of any Activity is created with 20% of the effort. Pareto Analysis is also used in Problem Management to prioritise possible Problem causes for investigation.

Participation rate
The number of incidents closed with a solution linked or cited, includes both creation and reuse of solutions

Partnership
A relationship between two Organizations which involves working closely together for common goals or mutual benefit. The IT Service Provider should have a Partnership with the Business, and with Third Parties who are critical to the delivery of IT Services. See Value Network.

Pattern of Business Activity (PBA)
A Workload profile of one or more Business Activities. Patterns of Business Activity are used to help the IT Service Provider understand and plan for different levels of Business Activity. See User Profile.

Percentage first contact resolution
Percentage of incidents resolved the support center on the first interaction. Used as a customer satisfaction indicator as well as an employee proficiency or process goal

Performance Management
The Process responsible for day-to-day Capacity Management Activities. These include Monitoring, Threshold detection, Performance analysis and Tuning, and implementing Changes related to Performance and Capacity.

Pilot
A limited Deployment of an IT Service, a Release or a Process to the Live Environment. A Pilot is used to reduce Risk and to gain User feedback and Acceptance. See Test, Evaluation.

Plan-Do-CheckAct
A four stage cycle for Process management, attributed to Edward Deming. Plan-Do-Check-Act is also called the Deming Cycle. PLAN: Design or revise Processes that support the IT Services. DO: Implement the Plan and manage the Processes. CHECK: Measure the Processes and IT Services, compare with Objectives and produce reports ACT: Plan and implement Changes to improve the Processes.

Policy
Formally documented management expectations and intentions. Policies are used to direct decisions, and to ensure consistent and appropriate development and implementation of Processes, Standards, Roles, Activities, IT Infrastructure etc.

Post Implementation Review (PIR)
A Review that takes place after a Change or a Project has been implemented. A PIR determines if the Change or Project was successful, and identifies opportunities for improvement.

Priority
A Category used to identify the relative importance of an Incident, Problem or Change. Priority is based on Impact and Urgency, and is used to identify required times for actions to be taken. For example the SLA may state that Priority2 Incidents must be resolved within 12 hours.

Proactive Problem Management
Part of the Problem Management Process. The Objective of Proactive Problem Management is to identify Problems that might otherwise be missed. Proactive Problem Management analyses Incident Records, and uses data collected by other IT Service Management Processes to identify trends or significant Problems.

Problem
A cause of one or more Incidents. The cause is not usually known at the time a Problem Record is created, and the Problem Management Process is responsible for further investigation.

Problem Management
The Process responsible for managing the Lifecycle of all Problems. The primary Objectives of Problem Management are to prevent Incidents from happening, and to minimise the Impact of Incidents that cannot be prevented.

Problem Record
A Record containing the details of a Problem. Each Problem Record documents the Lifecycle of a single Problem.

Procedure
A Document containing steps that specify how to achieve an Activity. Procedures are defined as part of Processes. See Work Instruction.

Process
A structured set of Activities designed to accomplish a specific Objective. A Process takes one or more defined inputs and turns them into defined outputs. A Process may include any of the Roles, responsibilities, tools and management Controls required to reliably deliver the outputs. A Process may define Policies, Standards, Guidelines, Activities, and Work Instructions if they are needed.

Process Control
The Activity of planning and regulating a Process, with the Objective of performing the Process in an Effective, Efficient, and consistent manner.

Process Manager
A Role responsible for Operational management of a Process. The Process Manager's responsibilities include Planning and co-ordination of all Activities required to carry out, monitor and report on the Process.

Process Owner
A Role responsible for ensuring that a Process is Fit for Purpose. The Process Owner's responsibilities include sponsorship, Design, Change Management and continual improvement of the Process and its Metrics. This Role is often assigned to the same person who carries out the Process Manager Role, but the two Roles may be separate in larger Organizations.

Product improvements (Number of RFEs accepted by product development)
The rate at which suggestions for product, documentation or service offering improvements are implemented by development, an indicator of influence.

Project
A temporary Organization, with people and other Assets required to achieve an Objective or other Outcome. Each Project has a Lifecycle that typically includes Initiation, Planning, execution, Closure etc. Projects are usually managed using a formal methodology such as PRINCE2.

Publish
When knowledge base articles have been written, checked and are ready for public consumption, go public! Let your customers be able to search, view and comment on what you've written.

Quality Assurance (QA)
The Process responsible for ensuring that the Quality of a product, Service or Process will provide its intended Value.

Quality Management System (QMS)
The set of Processes responsible for ensuring that all work carried out by an Organization is of a suitable Quality to reliably meet Business Objectives or Service Levels. See ISO 9000.

Question
"How/what/why....?". Any business knows this one. This is exactly the reason you need to embrace KCS. The sooner you start, the sooner you realize the benefits.

RACI
A Model used to help define Roles and Responsibilities. RACI stands for Responsible, Accountable, Consulted and Informed. See Stakeholder.

Rating
All knowledge should be subject to a rating by the consumer. When people search for information and are presented with a list of possible knowledge base articles, they should have the opportunity to rate the relevancy, content and quality of the suggested solution. The overall rating of the knowledge base article reflects an aggregate of how good the article is for a given search.

Ratio of known to new
New solutions created in the knowledge base vs. reuse of existing solutions

Release
A collection of hardware, software, documentation, Processes or other Components required to implement one or more approved Changes to IT Services. The contents of each Release are managed, Tested, and Deployed as a single entity.

Release and Deployment Management
The Process responsible for both Release Management and Deployment.

Release Management
The Process responsible for Planning, scheduling and controlling the movement of Releases to Test and Live Environments.

Release Unit
Components of an IT Service that are normally Released together. A Release Unit typically includes sufficient Components to perform a useful Function. For example one Release Unit could be a Desktop PC, including Hardware, Software, Licenses, Documentation etc. A different Release Unit may be the complete Payroll Application, including IT Operations Procedures and User training.

Reliability
A measure of how long a Configuration Item or IT Service can perform its agreed Function without interruption. Usually measured as MTBF or MTBSI. The term Reliability can also be used to state how likely it is that a Process, Function etc. will deliver its required outputs. See Availability.

Request for Change (RFC)
A formal proposal for a Change to be made. An RFC includes details of the proposed Change, and may be recorded on paper or electronically. The term RFC is often misused to mean a Change Record, or the Change itself.

Request Fulfilment
The Process responsible for managing the Lifecycle of all Service Requests.

Requirement
A formal statement of what is needed. For example a Service Level Requirement, a Project Requirement or the required Deliverables for a Process. See Statement of Requirements.

Resilience
The ability of a Configuration Item or IT Service to resist Failure or to Recover quickly following a Failure. For example, an armoured cable will resist failure when put under stress. See Fault Tolerance.

Resolution
The fix, work around or course of action that should be taken in order to address the issue that the client is experiencing. Each knowledge base article should clearly specify and delineate what resolutions are available.

Resolution capacity
How many incidents can the support organization handle in a period of time; indicators are incidents/month/analyst or average work time to resolve (work minutes, not elapsed time)

Resource
A generic term that includes IT Infrastructure, people, money or anything else that might help to deliver an IT Service. Resources are considered to be Assets of an Organization. See Capability, Service Asset.

Response Time
A measure of the time taken to complete an Operation or Transaction. Used in Capacity Management as a measure of IT Infrastructure Performance, and in Incident Management as a measure of the time taken to answer the phone, or to start Diagnosis.

Restore
Taking action to return an IT Service to the Users after Repair and Recovery from an Incident. This is the primary Objective of Incident Management.

Retire
Permanent removal of an IT Service, or other Configuration Item, from the Live Environment. Retired is a stage in the Lifecycle of many Configuration Items.

Return on Investment (ROI)
A measurement of the expected benefit of an investment. In the simplest sense it is the net profit of an investment divided by the net worth of the assets invested. See Net Present Value, Value on Investment.

Return on investment (ROI)
KCS allows you to solve cases quicker, solve more cases on the first point of contact, and improve overall employee and organizational efficiency.

Reuse
Refers to knowledge base articles that can be used over and over again. The principle of "Write once - use often" applies here. This is one of the key principles of KCS. The higher the "re-use" factor a knowledge base article has, the better it is. KCS administrators should monitor this statistics closely for changes and action it accordingly. Do not underestimate the value of "reuse". This is where it's at!

Reviewer
The role of the knowledge base article reviewer. This is a person who doesn't necesarily have the knowledge to write an article, but has the literery skills to know whether a knowledge base article is well written. It's their job to review, advise and correct knowledge base content.

RFE
Request for product enhancement.

Rights
Entitlements, or permissions, granted to a User or Role. For example the Right to modify particular data, or to authorize a Change.

Risk
A possible Event that could cause harm or loss, or affect the ability to achieve Objectives. A Risk is measured by the probability of a Threat, the Vulnerability of the Asset to that Threat, and the Impact it would have if it occurred.

Risk Assessment
The initial steps of Risk Management. Analyzing the value of Assets to the business, identifying Threats to those Assets, and evaluating how Vulnerable each Asset is to those Threats. Risk Assessment can be quantitative (based on numerical data) or qualitative.

Risk Management
The Process responsible for identifying, assessing and controlling Risks. See Risk Assessment.

Role
A set of responsibilities, Activities and authorities granted to a person or team. A Role is defined in a Process. One person or team may have multiple Roles, for example the Roles of Configuration Manager and Change Manager may be carried out by a single person.

Role
A role in KCS refers to the different position a person may play in the knowledge delivery process. Roles may include the following: Author, Reviewer, Technical consultant, Auditor and Administrator.

Rollout
Synonym for Deployment. Most often used to refer to complex or phased Deployments or Deployments to multiple locations.

Root Cause
The underlying or original cause of an Incident or Problem.

Root Cause Analysis (RCA)
An Activity that identifies the Root Cause of an Incident or Problem. RCA typically concentrates on IT Infrastructure failures. See Service Failure Analysis.

Scope
Each knowledge base article should clearly identify what it relates to, what products, platforms, operating systems etc it relates to

Search
Something a user does....a lot. When people search for knowledge, they are expecting answers.

Self service success
The percentage of time customers find what they need by using self-service (most often but not always use of the web).

Self-service use
The percentage of time customers use self-service before they open an incident.

Service
A means of delivering value to Customers by facilitating Outcomes.

Service Acceptance Criteria (SAC)
A set of criteria used to ensure that an IT Service meets its functionality and Quality Requirements and that the IT Service Provider is ready to Operate the new IT Service when it has been Deployed. See Acceptance.

Service Asset and Configuration Management (SACM)
The Process responsible for both Configuration Management and Asset Management.

Service Capacity Management (SCM)
The Activity responsible for understanding the Performance and Capacity of IT Services.

Service Catalogue
A database or structured Document with information about all Live IT Services, including those available for Deployment. The Service Catalogue is the only part of the Service Portfolio published to Customers, and is used to support the sale and delivery of IT Services. The Service Catalogue includes information about deliverables, prices, contact points, ordering and request Processes. See Contract Portfolio.

Service Continuity Management
Synonym for IT Service Continuity Management.

Service Contract
A Contract to deliver one or more IT Services. The term Service Contract is also used to mean any Agreement to deliver IT Services, whether this is a legal Contract or an SLA. See Contract Portfolio.

Service Design
A stage in the Lifecycle of an IT Service. Service Design includes a number of Processes and Functions and is the title of one of the Core ITIL publications. See Design.

Service Design Package
Document(s) defining all aspects of an IT Service and its Requirements through each stage of its Lifecycle. A Service Design Package is produced for each new IT Service, major Change, or IT Service Retirement.

Service desk
The Single Point of Contact between the Service Provider and the Users. A typical service desk manages Incidents and Service Requests, and also handles communication with the Users.

Service Improvement Plan (SIP)
A formal Plan to implement improvements to a Process or IT Service.

Service Knowledge Management System (SKMS)
A set of tools and databases that are used to manage knowledge and information. The SKMS includes the Configuration Management System, as well as other tools and databases. The SKMS stores, manages, updates, and presents all information that an IT Service Provider needs to manage the full Lifecycle of IT Services.

Service Level
Measured and reported achievement against one or more Service Level Targets. The term Service Level is sometimes used informally to mean Service Level Target.

Service Level Agreement (SLA)
An Agreement between an IT Service Provider and a Customer. The SLA describes the IT Service, documents Service Level Targets, and specifies the responsibilities of the IT Service Provider and the Customer. A single SLA may cover multiple IT Services or multiple Customers. See Operational Level Agreement.

Service Level Management (SLM)
The Process responsible for negotiating Service Level Agreements, and ensuring that these are met. SLM is responsible for ensuring that all IT Service Management Processes, Operational Level Agreements, and Underpinning Contracts, are appropriate for the agreed Service Level Targets. SLM monitors and reports on Service Levels, and holds regular Customer reviews.

Service Level Package (SLP)
A defined level of Utility and Warranty for a particular Service Package. Each SLP is designed to meet the needs of a particular Pattern of Business Activity. See Line of Service.

Service Level Requirement (SLR)
A Customer Requirement for an aspect of an IT Service. SLRs are based on Business Objectives and are used to negotiate agreed Service Level Targets.

Service Management
Service Management is a set of specialized organizational capabilities for providing value to customers in the form of services.

Service Management Lifecycle
An approach to IT Service Management that emphasizes the importance of coordination and Control across the various Functions, Processes, and Systems necessary to manage the full Lifecycle of IT Services. The Service Management Lifecycle approach considers the Strategy, Design, Transition, Operation and Continuous Improvement of IT Services.

Service Manager
A manager who is responsible for managing the end-to-end Lifecycle of one or more IT Services. The term Service Manager is also used to mean any manager within the IT Service Provider. Most commonly used to refer to a Business Relationship Manager, a Process Manager, an Account Manager or a senior manager with responsibility for IT Services overall.

Service Operation
A stage in the Lifecycle of an IT Service. Service Operation includes a number of Processes and Functions and is the title of one of the Core ITIL publications. See Operation.

Service Owner
A Role which is accountable for the delivery of a specific IT Service.

Service Package
A detailed description of an IT Service that is available to be delivered to Customers. A Service Package includes a Service Level Package and one or more Core Services and Supporting Services.

Service Pipeline
A database or structured Document listing all IT Services that are under consideration or Development, but are not yet available to Customers. The Service Pipeline provides a Business view of possible future IT Services and is part of the Service Portfolio which is not normally published to Customers.

Service Portfolio
The complete set of Services that are managed by a Service Provider. The Service Portfolio is used to manage the entire Lifecycle of all Services, and includes three Categories: Service Pipeline (proposed or in Development); Service Catalogue (Live or available for Deployment); and Retired Services. See Service Portfolio Management, Contract Portfolio.

Service Portfolio Management (SPM)
The Process responsible for managing the Service Portfolio. Service Portfolio Management considers Services in terms of the Business value that they provide.

Service Potential
The total possible value of the overall Capabilities and Resources of the IT Service Provider.

Service Provider
An Organization supplying Services to one or more Internal Customers or External Customers. Service Provider is often used as an abbreviation for IT Service Provider. See Type I Service Provider, Type II Service Provider, Type III Service Provider.

Service Request
A request from a User for information, or advice, or for a Standard Change or for Access to an IT Service. For example to reset a password, or to provide standard IT Services for a new User. Service Requests are usually handled by a service desk, and do not require an RFC to be submitted. See Request Fulfilment.

Service Strategy
The title of one of the Core ITIL publications. Service Strategy establishes an overall Strategy for IT Services and for IT Service Management.

Service Transition
A stage in the Lifecycle of an IT Service. Service Transition includes a number of Processes and Functions and is the title of one of the Core ITIL publications. See Transition.

Service Utility
The Functionality of an IT Service from the Customer's perspective. The Business value of an IT Service is created by the combination of Service Utility (what the Service does) and Service Warranty (how well it does it). See Utility.

Service Validation and Testing
The Process responsible for Validation and Testing of a new or Changed IT Service. Service Validation and Testing ensures that the IT Service matches its Design Specification and will meet the needs of the Business.

Service Valuation
A measurement of the total Cost of delivering an IT Service, and the total value to the Business of that IT Service. Service Valuation is used to help the Business and the IT Service Provider agree on the value of the IT Service.

Service Warranty
Assurance that an IT Service will meet agreed Requirements. This may be a formal Agreement such as a Service Level Agreement or Contract, or may be a marketing message or brand image. The Business value of an IT Service is created by the combination of Service Utility (what the Service does) and Service Warranty (how well it does it). See Warranty.

Serviceability
The ability of a Third Party Supplier to meet the terms of their Contract. This Contract will include agreed levels of Reliability, Maintainability or Availability for a Configuration Item.

Single Point of Contact
Providing a single consistent way to communicate with an Organization or Business Unit. For example, a Single Point of Contact for an IT Service Provider is usually called a service desk.

SLAM Chart
A Service Level Agreement Monitoring Chart is used to help monitor and report achievements against Service Level Targets. A SLAM Chart is typically color coded to show whether each agreed Service Level Target has been met, missed, or nearly missed during each of the previous 12 months.

Solution quality index
SQI index is based on adherence to criteria defined in the KCS Content Standard (see the KCS Practices Guide)

Stakeholder
All people who have an interest in an Organization, Project, IT Service etc. Stakeholders may be interested in the Activities, targets, Resources, or Deliverables. Stakeholders may include Customers, Partners, employees, shareholders, owners, etc. See RACI.

Standard
A mandatory Requirement. Examples include ISO/IEC 20000 (an international Standard), an internal security Standard for Unix configuration, or a government Standard for how financial Records should be maintained. The term Standard is also used to refer to a Code of Practice or Specification published by a Standards Organization such as ISO or BSI. See Guideline.

Standard Change
A pre-approved Change that is low Risk, relatively common and follows a Procedure or Work Instruction. For example password reset or provision of standard equipment to a new employee. RFCs are not required to implement a Standard Change, and they are logged and tracked using a different mechanism, such as a Service Request. See Change Model.

Status
The name of a required field in many types of Record. It shows the current stage in the Lifecycle of the associated Configuration Item, Incident, Problem etc.

Status Accounting
The Activity responsible for recording and reporting the Lifecycle of each Configuration Item.

Strategic
The highest of three levels of Planning and delivery (Strategic, Tactical, Operational). Strategic Activities include Objective setting and long term planning to achieve the overall Vision.

Subject matter expert
Every knowledge base article needs to be written by someone who has good knowledge on the subject. If your article consistently gets back feedback, send it back to this person for a re-write!

Suggest an article
Allow your clients, customers and other users of your knowledge system to be able to suggest an article.

Supplier
A Third Party responsible for supplying goods or Services that are required to deliver IT services. Examples of suppliers include commodity hardware and software vendors, network and telecom providers, and Outsourcing Organizations. See Underpinning Contract, Supply Chain.

Supplier and Contract Database (SCD)
A database or structured Document used to manage Supplier Contracts throughout their Lifecycle. The SCD contains key Attributes of all Contracts with Suppliers, and should be part of the Service Knowledge Management System.

Supplier Management
The Process responsible for ensuring that all Contracts with Suppliers support the needs of the Business, and that all Suppliers meet their contractual commitments.

Support cost as a percentage of total revenue
The ratio of support costs to total company revenue; used to normalize the cost of support in a dynamic environment. Other possible ways to normalize the support costs include against products shipped, licenses sold, customers subscribed (cross functional measure)

Symptom
A section of a knowledge base article that addresses an issue. The symptom is something that has happened to a customer. By defining what they might experience, you quickly gain their attention and direct them to your knowledge base article.

System
A number of related things that work together to achieve an overall Objective. For example: ❀ A computer System including hardware, software and Applications. ❀ A management System, including multiple Processes that are planned and managed together. For example a Quality Management System. ❀ A Database Management System or Operating System that includes many software modules that are designed to perform a set of related Functions.

Tactical
The middle of three levels of Planning and delivery (Strategic, Tactical, Operational). Tactical Activities include the medium term Plans required to achieve specific Objectives, typically over a period of weeks to months.

Take time
KCS takes time to implement and to succeed. If a knowledge article does not exist at the time of searching for it, take the time to make one, or at least start it. Get the key concepts down. An investment in time now will save much time later.

Target audience
Write knowledge base articles for an audience. Clearly specify this in the article itself so that your clients know if it is applicable to them.

Taxonomy
Referring to classifying things....as in classifying knowledge base articles with codes, issues, "applies to" etc. When you start making lots of knowledge base articles according to KCS principles, you're going to need a naming convention, or taxonomy.

Technical Management
The Function responsible for providing technical skills in support of IT Services and management of the IT Infrastructure. Technical Management defines the Roles of Support Groups, as well as the tools, Processes and Procedures required.

Third-line Support
The third level in a hierarchy of Support Groups involved in the resolution of Incidents and investigation of Problems. Each level contains more specialist skills, or has more time or other Resources.

Threat
Anything that might exploit a Vulnerability. Any potential cause of an Incident can be considered to be a Threat. For example a fire is a Threat that could exploit the Vulnerability of flammable floor coverings. This term is commonly used in Information Security Management and IT Service Continuity Management, but also applies to other areas such as Problem and Availability Management.

Threshold
The value of a Metric which should cause an Alert to be generated, or management action to be taken. For example "Priority1 Incident not solved within 4 hours", "more than 5 soft disk errors in an hour", or "more than 10 failed changes in a month".

Time to adopt new/upgraded products
Rate at which customers adopt new releases or products

Time to close
The elapsed time from incident open to incident closed

Time to proficiency for new employees and new technologies
The number of weeks or months required for an analyst to work with a high degree of independence; the learning curve

Time to publish
Time from initial issue discovery to the time information is available to customer

Time to resolution
See "average work time to resolve." Elapsed time from opening of an incident to offering an answer, fix, bypass or workaround

Total Cost of Ownership (TCO)
A methodology used to help make investment decisions. TCO assesses the full Lifecycle Cost of owning a Configuration Item, not just the initial Cost or purchase price. See Total Cost of Utilization.

Trend Analysis
Analysis of data to identify time related patterns.

Tuning
The Activity responsible for Planning Changes to make the most efficient use of Resources. Tuning is part of Performance Management, which also includes Performance Monitoring and implementation of the required Changes.

Turn it off an on again
Never under-estimate this option. It works. No need for a knowledge base article. Every IT worker knows this one.

Type I Service Provider
An Internal Service Provider that is embedded within a Business Unit. There may be several Type I Service Providers within an Organization.

Type II Service Provider
An Internal Service Provider that provides shared IT Services to more than one Business Unit.

Type III Service Provider
A Service Provider that provides IT Services to External Customers

UFFA
Use it, Flag it, Fix it, Add it. Take ownership of your knowledge. The people who use the knowledge, are accountable and responsible for maintaining and improving it, regardless of their position within the organization.

Underpinning Contract (UC)
A Contract between an IT Service Provider and a Third Party. The Third Party provides goods or Services that support delivery of an IT Service to a Customer. The Underpinning Contract defines targets and responsibilities that are required to meet agreed Service Level Targets in an SLA.

Unique
When a unique situation occurs, write an article for it!

Urgency
A measure of how long it will be until an Incident, Problem or Change has a significant Impact on the Business. For example a high Impact Incident may have low Urgency, if the Impact will not affect the Business until the end of the financial year. Impact and Urgency are used to assign Priority.

Use it
KCS works....but it involves a cultural change. Educate you staff about it. Teach them. Help them to help others.

User
A person who uses the IT Service on a day-to-day basis. Users are distinct from Customers, as some Customers do not use the IT Service directly.

User Profile (UP)
A pattern of User demand for IT Services. Each User Profile includes one or more Patterns of Business Activity.

Utility
Functionality offered by a Product or Service to meet a particular need. Utility is often summarized as "what it does". See Service Utility.

Value
Just one great knowledge base article can really save you time and effort.

Value on Investment (VOI)
A measurement of the expected benefit of an investment. VOI considers both financial and intangible benefits. See Return on Investment.

Variable Cost
A Cost that depends on how much the IT Service is used, how many products are produced, the number and type of Users, or something else that cannot be fixed in advance. See Variable Cost Dynamics.

Warranty
A promise or guarantee that a product or Service will meet its agreed Requirements. See Service Validation and Testing, Service Warranty.

Verified
The Consortium of Service Innovation verify software vendors that supposedly implement these principles.

Vision
A description of what the Organization intends to become in the future. A Vision is created by senior management and is used to help influence Culture and Strategic Planning.

Work Instruction
A Document containing detailed instructions that specify exactly what steps to follow to carry out an Activity. A Work Instruction contains much more detail than a Procedure and is only created if very detailed instructions are needed.

Workaround
Reducing or eliminating the Impact of an Incident or Problem for which a full Resolution is not yet available. For example by restarting a failed Configuration Item. Workarounds for Problems are documented in Known Error Records. Workarounds for Incidents that do not have associated Problem Records are documented in the Incident Record.

Workflow
Each knowledge base article should be subject to a workflow before it is made public. Define roles and responsibilities to ensure that every bit of knowledge is correctly authored, checked, approved and published.

Workload
The Resources required to deliver an identifiable part of an IT Service. Workloads may be Categorized by Users, groups of Users, or Functions within the IT Service. This is used to assist in analyzing and managing the Capacity, Performance and Utilization of Configuration Items and IT Services. The term Workload is sometimes used as a synonym for Throughput.

Vulnerability
A weakness that could be exploited by a Threat. For example an open firewall port, a password that is never changed, or a flammable carpet. A missing Control is also considered to be a Vulnerability.

References and sources

Thanks to everyone contributing to this book. Every friend and colleague at ComAround today or in the past as part of building and developing this experience and knowledge over the year. Thanks to Magnus Holmqvist (ComAround co-founder and friend) for your great feedback and recommendations to this book. Thanks to Greg Oxton, Executive Director, Center for Service Innovation (CSI) for reading the early draft and providing valuable recommendations. And last but not least, love to our families for your support and patience.

Sources:

KCS Practice guide – Consortium for Service Innovation http://www.serviceinnovation.org/included/docs/kcs_practicesguide.pdf

KCS Measurement Matters - Consortium for Service Innovation http://www.serviceinnovation.org/included/docs/kcs_benefitsandmeasures.pdf

KCS Principles and Core Concepts. The foundation of the methodology. http://www.serviceinnovation.org/kcs/

ITIL® V3 Foundation Course Glossary http://itil.it.utah.edu/downloads/ITILV3_Glossary.pdf

KCS - PRD Software. http://www.knowledge-centered-support.com/Glossary

www.ingramcontent.com/pod-product-compliance
Lightning Source LLC
LaVergne TN
LVHW021342070425
807938LV00009B/380